EVERYTHING
YOU NEED TO KNOW TO SURVIVE
THE WORLDWIDE CHASTISEMENT
WITH EARTHQUAKES ALL AROUND THE
WORLD STARTING THIS JULY 4TH, 2014

FRANCIS SLINSKY

Everything You Need To Know To Survive
The Worldwide Chastisement
With Earthquakes All Around The World
Starting This July 4th, 2014

by Francis Slinsky

Published by Mary's Way to Jesus Worldwide Apostolate, Inc.
Library of Congress ISBN 978-0-9905135-0-6

Cover by: Nancy Readinger

Author Non-Fiction Disclaimer:
What you are about to read is based on the real-life experiences
of the author and those individuals mentioned herein.
It is important to note that the last names of the individuals
mentioned within this entire book have been removed to protect their
personal privacy. All names, businesses, places, events and
incidents mentioned within this entire book are used
for educational purposes only.

To order additional copies of this book go to
www.marysway.net/shop
or send a check or money order for $29.95 (*includes shipping*)
per copy to:

Mary's Way
P.O. Box 33
Point Pleasant, NJ 08742

Printed in U.S.A

CHAPTER 1 1

Introduction to Mary's Way Worldwide Apostolate
      Promotion of Catholic Doctrine: "Our Lady Mediatrix of All Graces"
      Initial development of Mary's Way
            The Dream
            The Icon
            Pope John Paul II Blessing of the Sacred Icon

CHAPTER 2 3

Life of Father David
      Father David as a Child
      Padre Pio
      The Cure
      Stigmata Wounds
      Capuchin Priest
      Visions of The Blessed Mother
      Photograph of Little David with Padre Pio
      His Life with Padre Pio

CHAPTER 3 7

How Father David Found Mary's Way Worldwide Apostolate
      Dream from the Blessed Mother about the All-Protecting Brown Scapulars
      Photos of the Scapulars
      Padre Pio willed his personal belongings back to his Family.
      Father David's Donation of a Pair of Gloves and Personal Stole
      Meeting Bernadette
      Photos of the Gloves, Scab of Blood, Stigmata of Father David's Hands
      Photos of the Religious Articles

CHAPTER 4 19

Actual Accounts of Inexplicable Mystical Occurrences with Father David
      The Rainbow in Father David's Hospital Room
      Bernadette and Father David's Shopping Trip for Religious Articles
      Bernadette's Request of the Blessed Mother
      Father David under Attack
      The Scent of Roses Leads Straight to Father David
      Father David's Apparition with the Blessed Mother
      The Blessed Mother's Approval of Mary's Way and Francis Slinsky
      The Gold Glitter from the Angels
      The Blessed Statues of Padre Pio and Saint Benedict
      The Coming of Jesus
      The Gates of Hell Will Soon Be Opening

The White Horse in Cloud Formation of the Apocalypse
Vicka from Medjugorje
March 11, 2011

CHAPTER 5 53

Does the Devil Really Exist?
    Father David's Exorcism of 50 People
    The Description of the Picture of the Devil
    Photographs of The Blessed Mother and the Devil
    The Dream of Saint Louis de Montfort
    The Blessed Mother's Protection from the Devil

CHAPTER 6 57

Revelation from Blessed Mother to Father David
    The Filling of Houses with Saint Benedict Medals
    Sprinkling of Holy Water
    Burning of Bees Wax Candles
    The Chastisement is Coming
    The Three Days of Darkness
    Whoever Wears the Scapular will be Saved

CHAPTER 7 65

Angel Trumpets?
What the Bible has to say about Revelations and the Apocalypse
    Revelations Saint John the Apostle Received from God
    Who's in Charge?
    The White Horse of War
    The White Horse of War (6:1-2)
    The Red Horse of the Ethnic Strife (6:3-4)
    The Black Horse of Famine and Economic Crisis (6:5-6)
    The Pale Horse of Plague and Death (6:7-8)
    The Fifth Seal: The Tears of the Martyrs (6:9-11)
    The World Falls Apart at the Seams (6:12-17)
    Events Prior to the Final Outcome

CHAPTER 8 93

Our Lady of Revelations
    Pictorial Representation of Saint John's Gospel
    "A Woman Clothed with the Sun, and the Moon was under her
    Feet, and upon her Head a Crown of Twelve Stars".
    Description of the Photograph of the Blessed Mother

CHAPTER 9 99

All-Important Facts About Mary's Way Apostolate
 How It Began
 The Icon was completed on Christmas Day 1996
 as Mary's Gift to the Entire World

CHAPTER 10 101

Forty Vitally Important Facts and Dates about "The Miraculous Icon®"
"Our Lady Mediatrix of All Graces®"
 Her Eyes Are Always on You
 Painted by Josyp Terelya
 When the Icon was Revealed
 A Gift from the Blessed Mother to the World
 The Blessing of the Icon by Bishop Roman Danylak
 The Number 13
 The Feast of the Visitation
 The Display at Saint Peter's Basilica

CHAPTER 11 109

Amazing Information About "The 12 Way All-Protecting Brown Scapulars"
 The Dream
 Father David's Stigmata
 Offertory Masses By Father David
 Father David's Work with the Orphanages

CHAPTER 12 113

Three Days of Darkness
 Our Lord to Padre Pio

CHAPTER 13 117

Our Lady of La Salette
 The Vision of the Virgin Mary on Mount Sous-Les Baisses
 The Time of God's Wrath has Arrived

Photographs in this Book

1. The Miraculous Icon® was very specially painted in 1996, finished on Christmas Day, the 2000th Birthday of Jesus as Blessed Mother's Birthday Gift to the world through Mary's Way Worldwide Apostolate by Josyp Terelya (1945-2009), world renowned mystic and Marian visionary, chosen by Our Lady and the only person who could paint this Icon accurately!

2. Saint Pope John Paul II the Great personally blessed The Original Miraculous Icon with Mary's Most Powerful Role as our "Our Lady Mediatrix and Dispenser of all of God's Graces"! This historic private audience was in the Pope's personal office and library May 14, 1999 in the Vatican.

3. This photograph of then 3½ year old David shows Padre Pio lovingly talking to and praying for young David. Father David later recounted: "Padre Pio was praying for me." Padre Pio loved this little boy very much. David recalls what Padre Pio had said of him, "Why my child, you were greatly suffering like that for a long time!" *

4. TO THIS DAY, MORE THAN 55 YEARS LATER, FATHER DAVID STILL HAS THE ROSARY BEADS AROUND HIS HEAD, AS SHOWN IN THIS RECENT PHOTO taken by Francis Slinsky - Founder and Director of Mary's Way to Jesus Worldwide Apostolate. Father David, who is Francis Slinsky's personal Spiritual Director, told Francis that he (Father David) prays over 20 rosaries every day!

5. Father David in Medjugorje in 1999. When this photo was developed, the image of Jesus in the Divine Mercy appeared in it over Father David, which can be seen in the red and pale "Divine Mercy Rays", with the sun mysteriously setting at the 3 o'clock hour, over the Divine Mercy image, on this side of the mountain!

6. On August 5th, 2010 in the early AM hours, Father David had a dream in which the Blessed Virgin Mary appeared to him holding a brown Scapular with an Icon of Our Lady Mediatrix of All Graces on it that he had never seen.

7. Francis Slinsky, Director, found two scapular companies that agreed to work together on this "impossible task" to make our Scapulars ON OUR LADY'S BIRTHDAY, August 5th 2010 "The Feast Day of Our Lady of Snows"– TRULY, OUR BLESSED MOTHER'S BIRTHDAY GIFT TO THE WORLD - in these most needed times!

8. Each of our Scapulars requires over 2,000 very lustrous, silk damask threads, satin weaved three layers thick behind our two Icons on our Scapulars, under the world's finest, softest, most expensive brown woven wool – which go into making them The World's Finest Scapulars.

9. Saint Padre Pio's Actual Stole his favorite that he used during 12 to16 hours of hearing confessions. Also, the Most Miraculous Gloves of Padre Pio!

10. Padre Pio's Scab of Blood extremely miraculously appeared under his blessing hand glove out of nowhere! (Photo enlarged to show detail)

11. Photo taken in 2002 of Father David's Stigmata showing his left hand.

12. Photo taken November 2013 of Father David's left hand showing his Stigmata.

13. Photo taken November 2013 of Father David's Stigmata on his right hand.

14. Photo of Father David's hands after the healing service for 50 people with the blood oozing out from the pores in 2010.

15. Photo taken in 2010 of Father David's left hand showing his stigmata with oil first coming out.

16. Photo taken in 2010 of Father David's left hand showing his stigmata with blood.

17. In 2010, the angels sprinkled this gold glitter all over the religious articles Father blessed during the night.

18. Photo taken in 2010 of the gold glitter on the head of Mary's Statue by the Angels during the night - that Father blessed.

19. Photo taken in 2010 of thousands of pieces of silver and blue glitter perfectly shaped into a necklace around the neck of Baby Jesus by the angels during the night!

20. The statue of Mary that Father blessed in 2010 which is now exuding oil from the eyes, from the hands, and from the feet. And also "the pink small dots that appeared where coming out from the eyes" all with very sweet fragrances.

21. In 2012, the second of three statues of Padre Pio sweating blood for the great many sins of the world!

22. In 2012, the most miraculous statue of Saint Benedict which is bleeding, tearing, and showing stress veins on the hand for the many sins of the world after Father David had blessed the statue.

23. A picture of "The White Horse of the Apocalypse" in the sky from 2013, "When I finished praying the Rosary in front of a bush for 21 days, as Blessed Mother said, in front of the Monastery I asked God the Father, who I also speak to, 'When is my Beloved Jesus going to reappear?' God the Father said, "Look up my child." I looked in the sky, and there was The White Horse of the Apocalypse! The Second Coming of Jesus is going to happen very soon!."

24. Two boys in wheelchairs in Father David's orphanage.

25. Two children in wheelchairs with their arms crossed in Father David's orphanage.

26. A group of girls at therapy in Father David's orphanage.

27. One child in Father David's orphanage, feeding another orphan child.

28. Children eating at the orphanage

29. Photo of an orphan Father has been caring for who has a type of non-contagious leprosy. Once in the orphange, it is up to the orphan if they ever want to leave.

30. Boy receiving therapy at Father David's orphanage.

31. A boy from the orphanage in his crib.

32. Father David saying a healing prayer over a sick child who was miraculously cured soon after.

33. Father David comforting a small orphan child who was crying.

34. Father David at the orphanage with a child who passed away 2 weeks after this picture was taken.

35. The following pictures #35 through #49 have been specially blessed by Father David with his Liberating Blessing, Exorcism Blessing, and his Latin Blessing, and are available for purchase through our website and can be found throughout this book. Miraculous photograph of the true face of Jesus crying tears of blood for the great many sins of the world taken by Father David with permission - during his apparition of Jesus!

36. Actual photograph of the true face of the Blessed Mother crying for the sins of the world taken by Father David with permission - during his apparition of Mary!

37. Miraculous photo of Father David in Medjugorje with four miracles all around him.

38. Photo of Our Lady Mediatrix of All Graces Icon in Father David's Chapel with oil and serum continually pouring out of the Miraculous Icon!

39. Photo of Padre Pio with Blessed Mother revealing four miracles when the photo was developed.

40. During the Consecration, the Crucifix is miraculously bending towards Padre Pio.

41. At the Consecration, a glowing light miraculously emanating from the host held by Padre Pio.

42. Padre Pio Consecrating host and a second host miraculously appeared in the photograph.

43. Padre Pio miraculously appearing after his death, next to Father David's altar!

44. Padre Pio holding 3 ½ year old young David while praying for him.

45. Young David receiving a prayer card from Padre Pio at his First Holy Communion.

46. Padre Pio at the Consecration, during his last private mass, one month before he died.

47. Padre Pio consuming host at the end of the Consecration.

48. Saint Pope John Paul II blessing the original Mary Mediatrix of All Graces Icon.

49. Saint Pope John Paul II pointing out details in the Mary Mediatrix of All Graces Icon that was given to him as a gift.

50. Singularly unique photograph of Padre Pio hearing confessions at San Giovanni Rotondo in the 1950s.

51. Padre Pio praying the rosary two weeks before he died at San Giovanni Rotondo.

52. Padre Pio deeply immersed in Prayer for all of his spiritual children at San Giovanni Rotondo.

53. Padre Pio in front of pictures of Saint Francis and Saint Clare.

54. The Most Miraculous Gloves of Padre Pio at Mary's Way Worldwide Apostolate.

55. PADRE PIO'S 60 YEAR OLD BLOOD ON HIS BLESSING HAND GLOVE MIRACULOUSLY LIQUIFIED and a small drop of Blood dropped onto the very thick white paper it laid on AND WENT THROUGH 4 VERY THICK PAGES!

56. A VERY LARGE DROP OF BLOOD SERUM ALSO MIRACULOUSLY LIQUIFIED FROM PADRE PIO'S BLESSING HAND GLOVE and dropped onto the white paper it was on AND ALSO WENT THROUGH 4 VERY THICK PAGES!

57. The apparent GREAT HEAT FROM SAINT PADRE PIO'S DROP OF BLOOD (his blood was always extremely hot, over 127 F) CAUSED ALL 3 THICK PAGES TO WARP UP, TO BEND UP HIGH UNDER HIS SMALL DROP OF BLOOD!

58. Statue of Saint Padre Pio given to a benefactress by Father David. Upon being blessed by Father David, the statue started oozing blood!

59-62. This photograph of Our Lady Mediatrix of All Graces in The Miraculous Icon® was taken by Father David in his chapel. The Icon is next to his altar where he offers his Masses and prayers for people's intentions. These 4 Miraculous Signs from Our Lady Mediatrix of All Graces: (1) the Icon is miraculously exuding large quantities of oil, (2) blood serum, (3) both have very sweet fragrances, (4) and lights indicate that the Blessed Mother is answering Father David's and your prayers.

63. The most powerfully blessed and most protective Saint Benedict Medals for the three days of darkness and the upcoming chastisement with the all-powerful "liberating blessings" by Father David offered through Mary's Way for Father.

64. Icon and unique custom made "Mary's Frame" with museum quality fine art with icon on the finest canvas is available from Marysway.net

65. The brilliant white hot silhouette of the Blessed Mother in the air hovering over all the people with her rays of graces coming out of her in all directions, onto all the people, protecting them in Father David's evening healing service.

66. The actual photograph of the devil which Father David exorcised from a group of 50 people five years ago!

67. A photograph taken at Father David's monastery while praying to the Blessed Mother. This image of the Blessed Mother praying for the poor souls in purgatory with fire underneath her appeared when the photo was developed.

68. Mary's Way Worldwide Apostolate, Inc. website homepage photo.

69. Our Lady Mediatrix of All Graces Icon in Mary's Rays and Waves of Graces Iconic picture frame.

70. The Miraculous 12-Way All Protecting brown double Scapulars with Saint Benedict medals and crucifix.

71. Asteroid on a path towards the earth during the Three Days of Total Darkness for the coming chastisement.

This book is dedicated to:

My beautiful, loving wife, Joyce, "God's gift" to everyone who
comes in contact with her.
To my three sons, Francis, Shawn and Jason;
my daughters-in-law, Christine and Dayse
To my grandchildren, Catherine, Michael and Sean Patrick
To my parents, Frank and Elizabeth Slinsky, who are my role models
To my brothers and sister, Joseph, Alex and Julia
To all past and present employees and volunteers at
Mary's Way to Jesus Worldwide Apostolate, Inc.

I would also like to thank Josyp and Olena Terelya
for their patience, time, talent, and dedication
for more than the two years it took in creating
Our Lady of Mediatrix of All Graces Icon,
all four Marian Dogma Icons: Mother of God,
Perpetual Virginity, Immaculate Conception,
and Mary's Assumption into Heaven,
and the Saint Michael the Archangel Icon,
for Mary's Way Worldwide Apostolate, Inc.

I would like to especially thank my personal
Spiritual Director, Father David, for his prayers,
abundant blessings, and guidance throughout
the last several years, not only for my family and I,
but for all the patrons of Mary's Way Worldwide Apostolate, Inc.
Without Father David's spiritual guidance this book
would not have been possible.

PLEASE NOTE – Father David called Francis on Saturday morning June 21th 2014, and told him that Blessed Mother said that she is holding back the hand of her Son, further delaying the chastisement due to us. Our books were already being printed when this additional information from Father was given to Francis. Although no one knows the exact time and date of the chastisement, only God the Father knows, we still must prepare ourselves for these inevitable events to come.

As stated on the back cover of our book: Blessed Mother is holding back the hand of her Son, Jesus Christ, trying to save us from the upcoming chastisement! Blessed Mother said it will happen very soon!

Please note - This first edition of the book was printed as quickly as possible and there are some typographical errors and a couple of misstatements. Our second edition and the eBook edition have corrected these few errors.

CHAPTER 1
Introduction to Mary's Way Worldwide Apostolate

Mary's Way to Jesus Worldwide Apostolate, Inc. is a dynamic Worldwide Apostolate established in 1996 devoted to Jesus through His Most Holy Blessed Mother, Mary. An "Apostolate" is a group of people working together to promote a Doctrine of the Catholic Church which is *"Our Lady Mediatrix of All Graces"*! Mary's Way has been operating for over 16 years. Its' Founder and Director is Francis Slinsky.

The initial development of Mary's Way Worldwide Apostolate was inspired by one profound dream that the Director, Francis Slinsky had during the night in the year 1996. It was *"The Feast Day of Saint John the Baptist." Saint Louis de Montfort, the most Marian of all saints*, appeared to Francis in a dream in the United States. In the dream, Saint Louis was wearing his very distinct 17th. century priestly habit. Saint Louis de Montfort came down the aisle from the altar after Mass in a church named in honor of Saint Dominic. Our Lady said that one day through the Rosary and the Scapular she would save the world. In the dream, Saint Louis accurately foretold the creation and coming of the unique Sacred Icon *"Our Lady Mediatrix of All Graces"* to Francis who would surprisingly, soon become this Sacred Icon's caretaker.

The Icon was very specially painted for Mary's Way by Josyp Terelya (1945-2009), world renowned mystic and Marian visionary, chosen by Our Lady and the only person who could paint this Icon accurately! The Original Icon of "Our Lady Mediatrix of All Graces" was on stage and honored throughout the entire *"Vox Populi Mariae Mediatrici 1997 International Conference"* in Rome from May 30 through June 2, 1997. In attendance were Cardinals, Archbishops, Bishops, Priests, internationally renowned theologians and Marian leaders from 55 countries!

On May 14, 1999, Pope John Paul II specially blessed the original Sacred Icon of Our Lady Mediatrix of All Graces with Mary's very powerful role. This historic private audience was in the Pope's Personal Office and Library in the Vatican. After the Pope's discussion about this Sacred Icon, he pointed out details in the Icon! The Pope then said: "… Bring the Icon to my Chapel in my residence, and place the Icon next to the Altar for the Papal Mass and for prayers before Our Lady Mediatrix Icon!" This Papal Mass was concelebrated with 26 Archbishops and Bishops. (For more facts or information regarding the history of Mary's Way Apostolate and the Miraculous Icon of Our Lady Mediatrix of All Graces we humbly ask you to refer to the Chapters 8 - 11.)

Saint Pope John Paul II the Great personally blessed The Original Miraculous Icon with Mary's Most Powerful Role as our "Our Lady Mediatrix and Dispenser of all of God's Graces"! This historic private audience was in the Pope's personal office and library May 14, 1999 in the Vatican!

CHAPTER 2
Life of Father David

Father David as an infant was a very sickly child in Italy. His uncle, who was a priest working in Rome near the Vatican, heard about Padre Pio. He brought his nephew, young David, to Padre Pio hoping for a miraculous healing of his very severe brain tumor. After several surgeries on little David, the doctors didn't give much hope for young David to live. Padre Pio, upon seeing David, cried and cried over the severe condition of little David. David recalls what Padre Pio had said of him, "Why, my child, you were suffering like that for a long time!" "After much prayer over me," Father David said, "Padre Pio brought me, along with the Capuchin brothers and my uncle, closed the whole church, and prayed many hours of prayers over me, at a special Mass. After the Mass, Padre Pio came down to me. I was sitting down in the middle of church and he was praying with Jesus Christ! He scared me. I remember he was touching all around my head with his hands… I started feeling burning, like blood coming out from my head. It was very painful. I started healing, little by little…"

After his cure and for the next fifteen years, Young David was invited by Padre Pio's family to live with them near San Giovanni Rotondo. Padre Pio's sisters and nieces took care of little David. They were so very poor that they all slept on the floor, Father David reports. Young David was always with Padre Pio. Padre Pio very fondly asked young David to call him "Nonno" which means grandfather in Italian so young David always called Padre Pio Grandfather or "Nonno". David received his first holy communion from Padre Pio at the age of seven. When young David made his confirmation Padre Pio was David's sponsor. It was at this time that Padre Pio told David, "You are going to be just like me." Young David remembers asking, "In which way?", to which Padre Pio responded, "In every way."

Young David visited the monastery many times. David recounts how he told the Brothers in Padre Pio's Capuchin Monastery that he *"wanted to have his hair cut like Padre Pio!"* The brothers in the monastery did as young David asked. After David's hair was cut very short with little hair left on his head, they discovered the many bumps that circled around young David's head! The surprised brothers asked, *"Why do you have so many bumps on your head?"* In reference to the many small bumps that miraculously encircled David's shaven head! This happened when Jesus miraculously cured young David through the prayers of Padre Pio! The brothers counted the bumps and found as many bumps on young David's head as the beads on the rosary. David remembers them saying: *"PADRE PIO PUT ROSARY BEADS ALL AROUND YOUR HEAD!"* The brothers then told me *"that it meant that you are completely healed!"* Young David immediately ran to Padre Pio to thank him. Padre Pio smiled and said of young David's haircut *"NOW YOU LOOK JUST LIKE ME!"*

David became a Capuchin priest just like Padre Pio. David got the stigmata wounds of Jesus Christ, that Padre Pio told him he would be getting in 1969, one year after Padre Pio died. Father David's "Stigmata Wounds" of Jesus Christ were confirmed by Pope John Paul II and his Vatican Doctor. Saint Padre Pio very often appears to Father David in apparitions. Through Father David's prayers and Masses, many miracles are taking place. Father David was trained by the Chief Exorcist of the Vatican, who is the world's foremost Exorcist, Father Gabriele Amorth. He has performed over 100,000 exorcisms in the course of his very long ministry. He trained most of the exorcists in the world. Father Gabriele Amorth is Father David's personal spiritual advisor.

Father David sees our Blessed Mother just like Padre Pio did. Many miracles have happened when Father David prays to the Blessed Mother through images of her, for the intentions of people requesting masses to be said by him. Padre Pio, whose favorite prayer was the rosary, and who prayed unceasingly many rosaries all day and night long for over 50 years, and who was never without rosary beads in his hands, and who could read souls, was so very fond of David, and knew young David so very well, that when Jesus miraculously cured young David through Padre Pio's intercession, Jesus and Padre Pio permanently placed "a Crown of Rosaries; a Halo of Rosaries" around young David's head - which is still on Father David's head today.

* This photograph is of 3½ year old David taken at that time shows Padre Pio lovingly talking to young David. Father David later recounted: "Padre Pio was praying for me." Padre Pio loved this little boy very much. David recalls what Padre Pio had said of him, "Why, my child, you were suffering like that for a long time."

I asked Father about the photograph when he was a young boy when Padre Pio was holding him up. Was it him? He said, "Yes." Padre Pio's uncle was holding a young David up to Padre Pio's face. When Padre Pio saw him he said, "What a beautiful bambino", meaning baby. An attendant took the world famous picture. It was released when Padre Pio canonized a saint in 2002. It was in the Vatican archives. It is actually Father's picture which has been copyrighted through me, Francis Slinsky, but it went viral all over the internet. We will not press the issue. Anyone is welcome to use it. Father mentions that they gave him an 8 x 10 of that picture from the Vatican.

TO THIS DAY, MORE THAN 55 YEARS LATER, FATHER DAVID STILL HAS THE ROSARY BEADS AROUND HIS HEAD, AS SHOWN IN THIS RECENT PHOTO taken by Francis Slinsky - Founder and Director of Mary's Way to Jesus Worldwide Apostolate. Father David, who is Francis Slinsky's personal Spiritual Director, told Francis that he (Father David) prays over 20 rosaries every day!

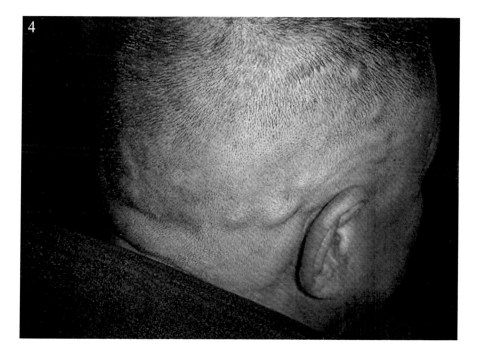

When I was with Father David on one of his rare visits to the United States (he comes about three or four times a year), I recall being in the backseat of a car with Father which was being driven by a friend. I asked Father about his head. I tried to get further information from Father about the damage of the skull, his head, and his brain. It was at that time that he said to me for the first time that "PADRE PIO WAS CRYING AND CRYING OVER MY SEVERE CONDITION."

Father David told me what he had said then and what Padre Pio said in return: "Why, my child, you were suffering like that for a long time!". What precious three and a half year old David said at that time really shocked me! Father David looked at me and said to me "At that time, I said to Padre Pio the little suffering that I have been doing now is very little compared to what Jesus Christ suffered for me and for everyone on the cross!" I was completely stunned and shocked. I could not believe what I had just heard about this, then three and a half year old "suffering saint"! This was a shocking statement, from a young boy who was obviously suffering a great deal, and is still suffering very much from his stigmata wounds and who still does not complain at all! But Padre Pio who was specially gifted by God: could read souls, and knew everything about people, knew exactly how greatly little David was suffering and for so long! As Padre Pio stated "Why, my child, you were suffering like that for a long time without telling anyone!" Padre Pio also knew at that time, how three and a half year old David was so wholly inspired by the Holy Spirit, that he related his suffering was little to nothing when compared with what Jesus suffered for all of us on the cross for our sins! It is no wonder that Padre Pio was taken so much by young David.

CHAPTER 3

How Father David Found Mary's Way Worldwide Apostolate

The information in this chapter is from some of the personal information my wife and I very carefully wrote down immediately after talking on multiple conversations with Father David for nearly four years, and also from talking to other people who know him very well. The information my wife and I gathered is from over 200 pages of notes in 3 notebooks.

The following information was given to me, Francis Slinsky, over the phone by Bernadette, a friend of Father David, whom Father had asked to call me, approximately four years ago in 2011.

Bernadette who had met Father David for the first time several months prior, called me because Father David, who lives in Italy, had asked her to order some of our Scapulars for him because Bernadette lives in the United States. Father David called Bernadette a few days after he had an astonishing dream from the Blessed Mother who presented to him in her outstretched hands the 12 Way All-Protecting Brown Scapulars of Mary's Way, which he had never seen before. The Blessed Mother, who actually appears live to Father David in apparitions, appeared to Father this time in a dream during the very same day, at the exact same hour, that Mary's Way's exquisite Scapulars finally were completed, after 10 years of searching for throughout the world for a company to make the extremely detailed scapulars.

In 1999, Father David made a holy pilgrimage with twenty of his Franciscan brother priests to Medjugorje. As they began to pray before the Statue of our Blessed Mother on Apparition Hill they became inundated with the very fragrant smell of roses, lilies and lilacs. Father David's fellow priests were taken aback by the powerful scent which engulfed them and became curious as to the origin of this very sweet aroma. They began to kneel and smell the plastic imitation flowers that were planted in devotion before the Blessed Virgin Mary statue on Apparition Hill. Father David stood at a distance in humility so as not to be discovered as the source of this nasal sensation. The aroma was emanating from the stigmata wounds on Father David's hands. When Father was content with the fact that his companions would not discover the origin of this heavenly sweet odor, he drew near and knelt before the statue of Blessed Mother. It was now the hour of Divine Mercy, 3:00 PM. As Father David knelt before the statue of Mary, he began to feel great warmth and had the feeling that something was happening. Father later told Francis, the Founder and Director of Mary's Way Apostolate: "Jesus was all round me! It was a beautiful feeling when the Divine Mercy rays were on my body. I felt a lot of joy. I was very happy to be there." Father further explained: "When I pray, I pray so hard - so intense – I feel the presence of Our Blessed Mother. It's such a good feeling."

The Franciscan Priests with Father David witnessed that the all light blue sky had suddenly burst into a pure white sky - that covered almost all of the clear blue sky! Only a small, jagged edged patch of blue sky can be seen in the upper left corner of a photo that one of the Franciscans felt inspired to take! When this photo was developed, the image of Jesus in the Divine Mercy appeared in it over Father David, which can be seen in the red and pale "Divine Mercy Rays", with the sun mysteriously setting at the 3 o'clock hour, over the Divine Mercy image, on this side of the mountain! Streams of Red and Pale Blue Divine Mercy rays can also be seen on Father David, angled out all around him. They can also be seen in all the shadows, on the base and pedestal of the statue, and on all 4 sides of the 10 foot statue.

Fascinated by this, the Franciscans contacted Pope John Paul II in 1999 and forwarded the picture to him. Pope John Paul II contacted Father David and invited him to a private audience in the Vatican. Father David humbly complied with Holy Father's request and went to the Vatican. Upon entering Holy Father's personal office, Pope John Paul II was taken aback by aroma of sanctity and asked Father David, "What is that sweet smell!? Father David replied, "It is you Holy Father"! Holy Father recognized that "the aroma of sanctity" was coming from Father's David's stigmata wounds on his hands and sent for the Vatican physician, who came, examined Father David's stigmata wounds and confirmed the wounds were not self-inflicted and were a genuine supernatural occurrence.

On August 5th, 2010 in the early AM hours, Father David had a dream in which the Blessed Virgin Mary appeared to him holding a brown Scapular with an icon of Our Lady Mediatrix of All Graces on it. He was not familiar with that icon. The day is of importance, because it was the feast day of "Our Lady of Snows", commemorating when the miraculous appearance of many inches of snow in the hot August summer heat in Italy, making the outline of a church Blessed Mother requested, built in her honor, in the fourth century.

This became the very first church dedicated to the Mother of God which eventually became Saint Mary Major Papal Basilica. This basilica would house the miraculous icon of Salus Populi Romani allegedly painted by Saint Luke which has been eventually linked to The Miraculous Icon® Our Lady Mediatrix of All of God's Graces®. Father David recognized the significance of these events and immediately contacted his spiritual director Father Amorth, who was the chief exorcist in Rome. After the description of the icon was given to him, Father Amorth identified that the icon that The Blessed Mother showed Father David in her outstretched hands on the Scapulars was Our Lady Mediatrix of All Graces. He reminded Father David of the document written about this icon and its owner Francis Slinsky by retired Cardinal Casaroli, Pope John Paul II's Cardinal Secretary of State Emeritus, in 1997. Father David had been given a copy of the letter when it was written, however he was not able to find it. The next morning after his Mass the letter was miraculously found next to Father David's altar on the credence table in Father's chapel; it was never there before.

6

Father David contacted Francis Slinsky and they met. Francis gave Father David an icon of Our Lady Mediatrix of All of God's Graces. Father David confirmed that this was the icon that Blessed Mother showed him on the Scapulars in his dream. Father David told Francis that: "Many miracles would come through these Scapulars with this Icon on them"

7

FRANCIS SLINSKY, Director, found two scapular companies that agreed to work together on this "impossible task" to make our Scapulars ON OUR LADY'S BIRTHDAY, August 5th 2010 "The Feast Day of Our Lady of Snows"– TRULY, OUR BLESSED MOTHER'S BIRTHDAY GIFT TO THE WORLD - in these most needed times! Each of our Scapulars required over 2,000 very lustrous, silk damask threads, satin weaved three layers thick behind our two Icons on our Scapulars, under the world's finest, softest, most expensive brown woven wool – which go into making them The World's Finest Scapulars. *

 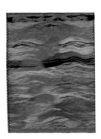  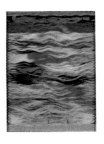

After Padre Pio's death, all 6 pairs of Padre Pio's gloves with his blood on them, which all had the very sweet fragrance of roses, lilies, and lilacs on them, and his favorite stole (that each of his family members personally hand-made a part of and then gave it to Padre Pio as a present for his 65th birthday), had been willed to his sister and his niece. Padre Pio used this stole which was his favorite stole when hearing confessions many hours a day during the last 15 years of his life. Padre Pio's blood and sweat, which are first class relics, are on the white neckband of the stole.

A few years after Padre Pio's death, Padre Pio's niece contacted Father David. Padre Pio's niece gave all of these religious items to Father David for his healing work. Father David recently donated a pair of Padre Pio's Gloves and Padre Pio's personal stole to me at Mary's Way to Jesus Worldwide Apostolate so that I could very reverently touch Padre Pio's Gloves and Stole and Scab of Blood to all the religious items people purchase from Mary's Way.

Saint Padre Pio's Actual Stole that he used during 12-16 hours of hearing confessions. It has Sacred First-Class Relic of his blood and sweat on the white inside neck band of the stole. Also, both the Most Miraculous Gloves of Padre Pio which has exuded blood and blood serum 52 times once for every week of the year, which shows that he will answer your prayers every day of the year.

Padre Pio's Scab of Blood extremely miraculously appeared under his blessing hand glove out of nowhere! – It was never on or in his 60 year old gloves. It most miraculously went through 60 years of time and space and landed under his glove.

Father David only gets the stigmata on his hands, except during Holy Week. However, all through last year's Lent and all through this year's Lent he had the stigmata. He gets the full stigmata (the full stigmata, all the wounds of Christ's passion, on his hands, foot and side, with whipping marks on his back, the knees and elbows bleeding and raw, the head bleeding in the same way as Jesus' bled from the crown of thorns) Father gets this throughout Holy Week and on Good Friday. It gets more intense on Good Friday to the point that he is bedridden. He told me once that he had to have a blood transfusion because he lost so much blood and was afraid for his life. I asked Father this Lenten Season why he was getting the stigmata from the beginning of Lent instead of just during Holy Week. He said, "Because of the many sins of the world." That is a very terrible, awesome sign.

Father David gets the stigmata during the year on his hands only, because he is the head of two orphanages with 505 abandoned children. He also now has just opened a home for terminally ill patients who are dying in their last stages of cancer and AIDS. There are 40 adults in that. That is Father's life work to rescue the children from pure death every evening and run the orphanages. He has many priests, religious brothers and religious sisters to assist him in running the two orphanages. He goes out in the morning rescuing children from the gutters and feeding the homeless in the morning and night time. Father is busy from 6 am to 10 pm with such a full schedule. This is the reason he does not have the full stigmata, like Padre Pio. This is because he is out in the world functioning and this is something that the people of the world don't see.

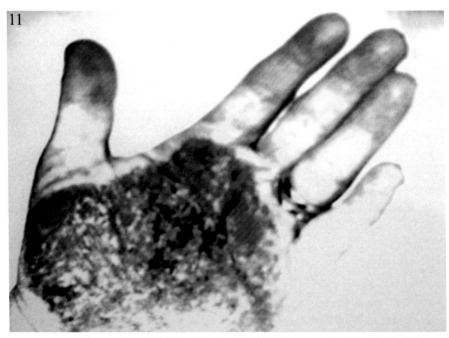

Photo taken in 2002 of Father David's Stigmata showing his (left) hand.

When Bernadette met Father David for the first time she told me that Father David had the stigmata and that she could smell the very sweet fragrance of roses, lilies and lilacs. Bernadette saw blood serum and oil coming out of the back of his hands every day. She also told me that "Saint Padre Pio and the Blessed Mother appear to Father David often. Sometimes Jesus appears to Father David also. There have been a lot of miracles wherever Father David goes!"

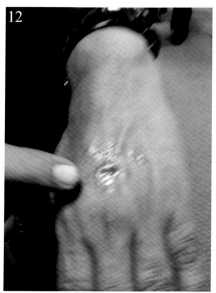

Photo taken November 2013 of Father David's left hand showing stigmata.

Photo taken November 2013 of Father David's Stigmata showing his right hand.

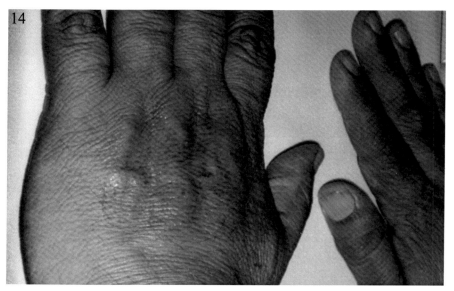

Photo of Father David's hands after the healing service for 50 people with the blood oozing out from the pores in 2011.

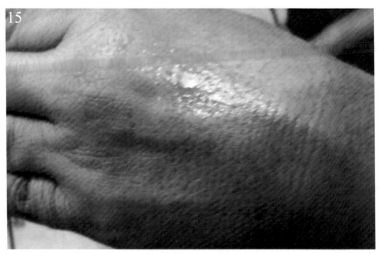

Photo taken in 2010 of Father David's left hand showing stigmata.

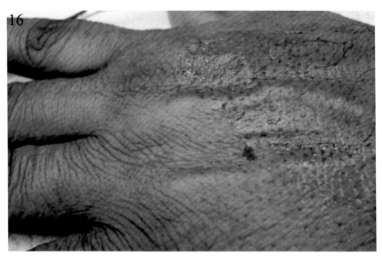

Photo taken in 2010 of Father David's left hand showing stigmata.

When Bernadette met with Father David in his country, Bernadette and her friend Gloria went shopping with Father for some religious articles. Bernadette told me: "We bought many religious articles. He put them on the table, and made a kind of altar in one of the nearby rooms in the hotel we were staying at. Father blessed them and prayed over them that evening. Then we all went to our regular hotel rooms. The next morning I heard a commotion in the hallway. I went back to that locked hotel bedroom with the hotel's very excited cleaning maid. When Father and I and the cleaning maid went into that locked bed room there was gold glitter all over the religious articles on the table.

Father David said that the angels sprinkled this gold glitter all over them during the night! My friend Gloria and I did not see any angels. We were asleep all that night. The hotel's cleaning woman was the first one to witness the gold glitter in that locked hotel room earlier that morning. She also very excitedly, shockingly told us about the big rainbow which she saw that stretched across top of the inside of that large bedroom from one corner of the room to the other corner! The cleaning maid was afraid to go back into that hotel room!

Bernadette and Father went shopping again for more religious items the next day. Regarding the gold glitter that appeared the day beforer, Bernadette told me she wrote a letter to the Blessed Mother using the hotel's stationery. She said "I took a picture of the empty letter on hotel stationary, and folded it in half, lengthwise, so that when the glitter would come down again I can catch everything." She continued "I secretly asked Blessed Mother that if this is real, if Father David is real, please also send me blue glitter! No one knew this. I did not tell Father David or my friend Gloria anything about this. I did not tell anyone!"

"Father again blessed and prayed over the new religious articles we just purchased that day. We returned to our hotel rooms that evening. The next morning I was very shocked and very surprised to find on the half folded hotel stationery that there was blue glitter and also silver glitter, and gold glitter on my religious articles and the other religious articles we just purchased. Obviously this was from Blessed Mother and the angels! *I took pictures of the gold glitter and the absolutely stunning, perfectly shaped, silver glitter necklace that the angels made around baby Jesus' neck made entirely from hundreds of silver glitter!*

About a year and a half later in 2012, when I spoke to Father David in person about Bernadette, he told me that Bernadette had the gold analyzed by a jeweler and he found it to be very, very old unusual gold!

Bernadette told me that, "when Father did a healing service in a prayer group two years earlier, the prayer group was infiltrated by darkness and one of the leaders of the group gave Father what was supposed to be a relic from a saint. It was not a saint's relic. I believe it was part of an evil deceased person. The spirit of that evil deceased person or something affected Father for weeks. He was not feeling well for weeks because of this. Being Father is such a holy person he's always being attacked and that is why he really needs the scapulars from Mary's Way!" Father asked, "Can you ask Francis to send the Scapulars right away because I'm being attacked every day?"

Bernadette told me, "Father David said to tell you that we are really, really happy that we connected with you. Thank you for the Icon T-shirts and the Icons of our Lady Mediatrix of all Graces you sent to him. Father felt a lot of energy from the Icons. When he put his hand on them they became really hot Father said!"

Bernadette continued "When I was with Father in a hotel room, we set up an altar, we put some pictures of my relatives and some petitions on the table. My friend Gloria placed a picture of her family on the table. The next morning Gloria handed a picture over to Father David and Father put the picture on his palm and prayed over it. The photograph became very hot to the touch. Father said that the woman there in the picture had something wrong with her brain, her throat, and her stomach! She also had breast cancer. I, (Bernadette) did not know anything about it. I only knew she had a breast problem. When Bernadette returned home in the United States, Bernadette did some research and came to find out that the woman had brain cancer, and also something wrong with her throat and other things". Father prayed over the relative's picture. Gloria's relative went to her doctor for a CAT Scan sometime after that. Everything cleared up. So it seems that Father can do healings from pictures also".

Please Note: Mary's Way Worldwide Apostolate cannot accept any photographs, pictures or religious items in the mail to be send to Father David. If you would like Father David to say Masses for you and your family, you could arrange that by your going to http://www.marysway.net/730-masses-by-stigmata-priest-for-intentions.

Bernadette said, "We set up a small altar in the hotel room, and each of the statues that Father blessed the day before were now exuding oil from the eyes, from the hands, and from the feet, and it was like pink small dots that appeared where coming out from the eyes. When I first arrived at the hotel that Father stayed at so we could visit him, I did not have the room number. I actually followed the smell of roses down the long hallway to find Father's hotel room right up to his door which had the strongest scent of roses! When

I saw Father I noticed that there was blood and oil coming out from the back of his hands. I could see that there was a little hole in the back of his hands. When I got back to the United States the scent followed me. The day before we left to go back to the United States, we took our religious items from the altar we set up and put them in our hotel room. I set it on the nightstand. It was still exuding oil and also those pink dots on the veil and it smelled like roses. I still have one of them left on the eyes. I hand carried the statue with me on the plane, returning back to the United States".

CHAPTER 4
Actual Accounts of Mystical Occurrences with Father David

"On March 17, 2011 Father David went to see a doctor in a hospital for a thorough checkup. He was in the hospital for a couple of days for various tests. A nurse in the hospital reported that a rainbow appeared in the consulting room where Father was and it stayed there for a week! So many nurses and doctors and hospital visitors came up to that floor to see the rainbow that was in the room where Father was, that they had to seal the room off to stop people from coming!"

Father David told me that Blessed Mother said to him in one of his apparitions people need to pray much more often. Blessed Mother said to Father "my Son is very sad because he has been much offended by abortions. The world doesn't want to pray the rosary. People do not want to pray the rosary. They do not fast anymore. They need to pray the family rosary together." Three years ago Father David became my personal Spiritual Director. The Blessed Mother told Father David that "Francis' work is very important. Francis is bringing many souls back to my Son!"

On Father's Day June 17, 2012 my wife and I met with Father David and with a very devout, holy woman that I knew for some time. Blessed Mother had asked her to ask me (Francis) to introduce her to Father David. Blessed Mother's exact humble words to this woman were: *"PLEASE ASK FRANCIS IF IT IS OKAY WITH HIM, COULD HE PLEASE INTRODUCE YOU TO FATHER DAVID?"* The woman, who was a patron of Mary's Way Apostolate, also told me about the many miraculous photographs she had taken. I (Francis) asked Blessed Mother to give me a Miraculous Sign that this is true. Blessed Mother gave me the miraculous signs that I asked from her to prove to me that Blessed Mother wanted me to introduce this woman to Father David.

This very devout woman, who in deep humility wishes to remain anonymous, e-mailed us many of the miraculous photographs she had taken at Blessed Mother's request and all the messages and revelations that the Blessed Mother gave her so that I could give them to Father David. I made 8 inch by 10 inch copies of each of her miraculous photographs and printed out all the messages she e-mailed to me for this meeting and put each of them into clear plastic sheet protectors, and then put them into three binders. I made one 3 ring loose leaf binder for Father David, one for the Visionary, and one for my wife and I, for this all day meeting.

In attendance were Father David, the woman visionary, and her secretary who wrote down everything that was said at this important meeting. She gave all this to her spiritual director in the United States and also to her spiritual director in Rome. My wife and I also received a copy.

Father David brought his own flexible folder holding dozens of photographs to show the four of us at the meeting. When Father opened up his 8½ inch by 11 inch folder what was trapped inside dozens of clear plastic sheet protectors was truly astonishing! There were many thousands of tiny pieces of very bright gold glitter trapped inside the clear plastic sheet protectors on top of all of Father David's photographs! They began to fall onto the large conference table in the private conference room I rented at the hotel for this special occasion. Father David was not at all surprised upon seeing this. He very simply said: *"Oh, the angels put them there"*.

Father David then turned the binder holding dozens of miraculous photographs upside down and proceeded to shake the binder so that the many pieces of gold glitter fell all over the conference table! The woman visionary was so startled, so shocked, as were my wife and I to see all this. The woman visionary (who is in her 50's) uncontrollably, very excitedly said: *"OH FATHER! OH FATHER! THIS IS SO WONDERFUL! SO WONDERFUL! I CAN'T BELIEVE THIS. I SIMPLY CAN'T BELIEVE THIS." She then knelt down on both knees and said, like a little school girl "FATHER, FATHER PLEASE SPRINKLE THE GOLD DUST ON ME. SPRINKLE IT ON MY HEAD, ON MY HAIR, SPRINKLE IT ALL OVER ME!"* Father then did as she asked. He picked up the thousands of pieces of gold glitter that were on the conference table and sprinkled it all over the visionary's head and hair. It was like seeing someone just coming out of a wedding when rice is thrown at the bride, landing all over the bride.

My wife and I were so taken by this, we also asked Father David to sprinkle the angel's gold glitter on our head and hair also. We individually knelt down in front of Father and he sprinkled the thousands of pieces of gold glitter all over us! We were all like little children again! It was such a startling development. It was incredible. I wish we had videotaped it. (Can you imagine the surprised look on the many hotel guests as we three walked out of the conference room, through the crowded hotel lobby, past the crowded front desk, and onto the elevators, with thousands of sparkling gold glitter pieces in our hair and on our clothes being followed by a very holy, priest/monk dressed in his habit with a smile on his face?)

The most startling development happened the day before all of this. My wife and I arrived at the hotel a day ahead of the visionary and her secretary. We met with Father David alone. The hotel manager was the only one who had the key to the small private conference room that I rented for the occasion. We went to the front desk and met the hotel manager, who took us to the small private locked conference room. He unlocked the door and there, to our great surprise and delight, there were two, exquisite, 12 inch lifelike statues, one of Saint Padre Pio and another of Saint Benedict. Father David said that he had brought them with him to give to my wife and I as gifts for us to take back with us to our Mary's Way to Jesus Apostolate in New Jersey. There was nothing out of the ordinary about these statues, except that they were very beautiful and very lifelike.

Father prayed over each one of them in Latin for several minutes. He then brought out some holy water that he had in a small plastic container, and blessed both statues. He also prayed over and blessed my wife and I. We spent the next three hours talking with Father in that conference room. We then went to our individual rooms. At 9 o'clock the next morning, my wife and I met Father, the visionary, and the visionary's secretary in the hotel lobby. We all had breakfast together in the hotel. After breakfast we went to the front desk to see the hotel manager again. We asked him to unlock the conference room, which had been locked up all night. He was the only person in the hotel with the key to the conference room. My wife was the first one to enter the conference room, and the first one to discover *THREE WONDERFUL MIRACLES HAD OCCURRED AFTER FATHER DAVID BLESSED THE STATUES!* My wife went in, then Father David entered, then the visionary, I followed the visionary, and the visionary's secretary was last. We all then saw the three miracles!

THE FIRST MIRACLE: THERE IS NOW BLOOD SERUM ALL OVER THE FACE OF THE SAINT PADRE PIO STATUE - just on his face and nowhere else – after Father David blessed the statue! It was not there before! This is an indication of Jesus' suffering at the Garden of Gethsemane, sweating blood for the great many sins of the world now. The Padre Pio statue is sweating blood on the face, similar to what Jesus suffered at Gethsemane.

My wife then looked down at the other statue at the other end of the long conference table and saw:

THE SECOND MIRACLE: THE SAME BLOOD-LIKE SUBSTANCE WAS COMING FROM THE HEAD OF THE LIFELIKE SAINT BENEDICT STATUE – after Father David blessed the statue! The blood-like substance was coming out of his bald head in 3 to 4 places. Saint Benedict was the first to develop the monastic rules for all priests in 530 A.D.

THE THIRD MIRACLE SAINT BENEDICT'S LEFT HAND ON THE STATUE, THE HAND THAT HOLDS HIS STAFF WITH HIS CRUCIFIX ON IT WHICH WARDS AWAY ALL EVIL WITH THE SAINT BENEDICT CRUCIFIX ON IT, ACTUALLY SHOWS LIFELIKE STRESS VEINS ON HIS LEFT HAND ONLY – for the many sins of the world after Father David blessed the statue! These miraculous statues of Saint Padre Pio and Saint Benedict are now at our Apostolate and can been seen on our website at www.marysway.net.

Blessed Mother and Jesus appear to this woman visionary very often. Father David, my wife, and I now know this holy woman very well. We have seen her many times. She told us this astonishing account and showed Father David, my wife, and I many miraculous photographs which Blessed Mother asked her to take in Fatima, Lourdes, Medjugorje, Spain, and in Our Lady of Grace Capuchin Church in San Giovanni Rotondo, Italy, where Padre Pio received the Stigmata proving her statement to us *"THAT JESUS WAS COMING SOON". THAT THE APOCALYPSE IS LIKELY COMING SOON! "THE GATES OF HELL WILL SOON BE OPENED"!*

She showed us dozens of photographs of many Crucifixes with real blood and real tears coming out of Jesus, with lifelike veins in the stomach of Jesus appearing in the photos but not on the actual Crucifixes and statues of Jesus. There are also many tracks of tears in the photos of the Crucifixes which are not on the original Crucifixes. She gave me photographs of statues of Jesus at the Scourging Pillar with real blood and real tears coming out of the Jesus, and many other astonishing Crucifixion scenes! At Fatima where she also took pictures, "Our Blessed Mother said to me (her) 'Take a picture of Francisco's grave' She answered: "Take a picture of the grave?" Blessed Mother responded: "Yes, my child, take a picture of the grave." When I took the picture of the grave, the 'Light of God' that Francisco spoke about just before he died, miraculously appeared in the photo. It looks like 'The Eye of God' with the pupil of the eye and the iris of the eye! It also looks like a Monstrance! Also Francisco was in that photograph standing near his grave! When I took a picture in 'Saint Michael's Cave' in Fatima, a very bright blue light in the shape of a ball miraculously appeared which I was able to take a picture of. The bright blue light got bigger and bigger and said to me "I am Michael the Archangel," and flew at me, clung to me, lifted me inches off the ground. I felt my shoes lift off the floor!"

This very close friend of Father David gave me all of these incredible photographs which are described here. This very devout humble woman said to me, "When I finished praying, I asked God the Father: 'when is my beloved Jesus going to reappear on earth for the judgment'? God the Father said, 'Look up my child'. I looked up into the sky, and there was a perfect, fully formed white horse made entirely of clouds: with the perfectly formed all white head, face, eye, neck, body, feet, and tail which is in the book of revelations: that when Jesus returns to earth, he will return on a white horse!

23

"When I finished praying the Rosary in front of a bush for 21 days, as Blessed Mother said, in front of the Monastery I asked God the Father, who I also speak to, 'When is my Beloved Jesus going to reappear?' God the Father said, "Look up my child." I looked in the sky, and there was the white horse, Jesus is going to return on in the Apocalypse. Because of the numbers falling off the watch – meaning we are out of time – and because God the Father gave me the sign in the sky of the perfectly formed horse-tail, feet, and so on – Jesus is returning in the Apocalypse. WE ARE OUT OF TIME! We are very close to major world changing events."

My wife and I met with Father, when he flew in and visited for 3 days in the United States, Father said to me, "Did you bring your bathing suit?" I said "No, Father, but I have a change of clothes in my room". He said "I'm going to 'consecrate you'. You are going to be a 'consecrated son' of Padre Pio. We're going to dunk you in the hotel pool, just like a Baptist!" Father prayed over me in Latin for about 15 minutes. It felt like an out of this world experience; like I was out of the realm of the physical and into the spiritual. Then Father did the same for my wife.

The woman visionary is a client of Mary's way. She often orders religious items from Mary's Way's Online Store. Blessed Mother most humbly asked the woman visionary to meet with me (Francis). I said yes and so we were with Father and the woman visionary for 2 days. Father had profoundly blessed me, my wife, the woman visionary and her recording secretary. The next day the woman visionary spoke to Father and told him that night she had excruciating pains in her hands and could not sleep. She showed us her hands and there was a red mark about the size of ½ a dime in diameter on each of her hands. Because she sees Blessed Mother, she knew in her heart and she said, "Father, I think I am starting to get the stigmata. Could you tell me? It looks that way. And I am in such pain." Father said, "Yes, you are starting to get the stigmata."

   I had been with Father about 2 1/3 years ago and he never ever complained about the pains in his hands or the stigmata. He has a wonderful, jovial personality. Father is very funny, humorous, endearing, and kind. He never once complained about any pain. He said to the woman visionary, "It burns, doesn't it?" She said, "Oh Father, the burning is so severe. My hands are on fire. I can't stand it. It is so severe." That told me that Father has always suffered from the burning of the stigmata, but never ever complained because of the saint that he is. The highest Cardinals in Rome called him a "living saint".

   The woman visionary indeed over the next several months continued to relay to me that the pain was getting more intense and there was a swelling in her hands, too. She voluntarily emailed me the pictures of her hands. The hands could not be identified as woman's hands. They were so severely swollen and red. So the stigmata which started the day after meeting Father, had gotten much more severe and more pronounced within the next 6 to 12 months.

   When I was with Father in a church in New Jersey, he was in deep meditation for 15 minutes in front of a magnificent crucifix. We left the church. Our car was in a remote part of the church's parking lot, we were with a woman benefactor; Father was walking briskly ahead of us. Even with the pains of the stigmata he was walking very fast ahead of us. Suddenly, the sweet fragrance of roses, lilies, and lilacs filled the air. I called, "Father, Father, Father, do you have the stigmata now?" He just humbly shook his head. We caught up to Father to look at his hands and the woman was speechless and her knees buckled. She almost collapsed. She was so shocked and taken by this. She said, "Oh, Francis, what a privilege to see this!" A great deal of oil profusely flows from each of Father David's many pores in his hands, prior to getting the sacred stigmata which are the wounds of Jesus Christ on his hands. The oil also has the very sweet fragrance of roses, lilies, and lilacs. Immediately after, Father receives the sacred stigmata on his hands

   We took photos and they are on our website. These are the recent photos from November of 2013. When Father is in deep prayer and deep meditation before the crucifix is when he gets the stigmata. Padre Pio was different. He always had the stigmata. He always prayed the rosary. I don't pretend to know why

Padre Pio always had the full stigmata 100% of the time. But in Father's case, he is the directly linked to Padre Pio. Padre Pio thought of Father David as if he was a grandson. That is how personal their relationship was.

However, this year and last year, Father David got the full stigmata starting at the beginning of Lent! I asked "Father, why are you getting the full stigmata well in advance of Holy Week?" He said "Because of the many sins of the world." It's a very terrible awesome sign.

Father David doesn't always have the stigmata, when he gets the stigmata during the year it's in his hands only, because he is the head of two orphanages with 505 abandoned, orphaned children. He also has now opened a home for terminally ill patients. Those persons have the last stages of cancer and last stages of AIDS. There are 40 adult patients.

This is Father's life's work; to rescue the children from sure death and to run the orphanages. He goes out in the morning and evening rescuing children from the gutters.

And then he feeds the homeless bringing them food in the morning, afternoon and evening. He is busy from 6 am to 10 pm.

Father told me to call him in the evenings because he is so busy. "I leave at 6 o'clock in the morning. I look for the kids in the street who are hungry. They are abandoned and live in the sewer systems. They inhale the fumes from the sewers. I have to look for them in the heaters of the hotels. They're sleeping on papers; they're sleeping on hot ventilation ducts. I've been fighting with the government about this. They say 'It is not our problem', I say 'Yes, it is your problem because these children belong to you and me'. The government only wants to enrich itself".

Father explained to me, how he goes out every evening to the place where the abandoned street children live. They group together in the sewers with the terrible stench of the rotten food and sewer gases. They keep warm by the heat of the steam coming from the sewers. Father always finds one or two children there.

He also mentioned, there is a river with a bridge, and the parents who don't want their children, newborns and so on, throw them from the bridge into the water to drown. They also throw them (the children) off the riverbank and a few land in the dirt and mud, and Father walks the length of the river for many miles and hears the cries of the infants dying of starvation and cold on the riverbank. He brings them back and baptizes them and brings them to the hospital for immediate care. Sometimes they die within one or two days, sometimes in his arms as he is baptizing them. Every night!

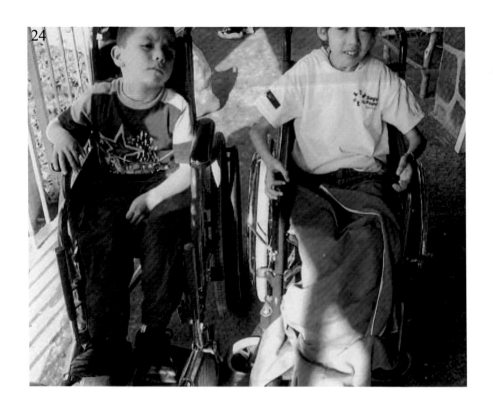

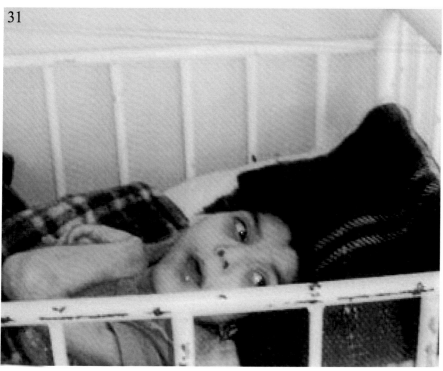

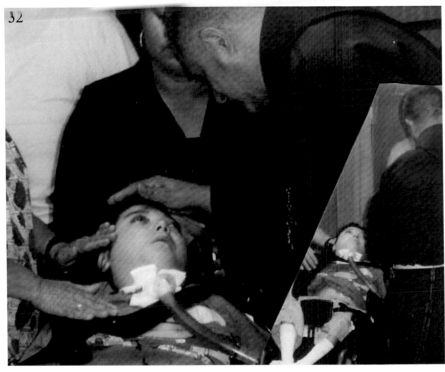

Father David told his spiritual director, Father Amorth, the chief exorcist of the Vatican, about the dream of the Blessed Mother, and Our Lady Mediatrix of All Graces scapulars. He reminded me "Don't you remember when Cardinal Casaroli told me, 'A lot of people will be saved with the Mary's Way Scapular'?".

Blessed Mother said to Father David, "You will be protected and saved, whoever wears the scapular".

Two years ago, Father David said, "Vicka (Medjugorje) calls me every week, sometimes twice a week, we're very good friends". She asks for his prayers. Vicka has a brain tumor and has very bad headaches. Blessed Mother said to Vicka, "Be prepared. Three days of darkness is coming soon".

The Blessed Mother told Vicka that the letters MIR would appear in the sky all over the world, probably in cloud formations. MIR (in Medjugorje) means "peace". She also took Vicka there are going to be very bad earthquakes; very, very bad. "Houses will be protected. Do not be afraid, I will remain with you. Pray the rosary, pray the Saint Michael prayer. There will be a lot of evil in the streets, everywhere in the world".

I interpret that to mean that when the gates of hell are open, when the demons are released, neighbor will turn against neighbor and there will be killing and murders in the streets (I interpret this personally), worldwide revolution, brother against brother, neighbor against neighbor. The sign of the cross will be in the sky.

Father said, "I prayed so much last night, I prayed to Divine Mercy. Divine Mercy appeared to me in Medjugorje; a huge light over my head." When evil attacks, pray the Saint Michael prayer 20 times.

I gave Father prayer cards, which he distributed to people in hospitals and streets and churches. When he blessed the prayer cards, I was with him, he put his hand on the prayer card itself, he then put the prayer card into my hand, it was very hot, I almost dropped it because it was so hot.

Father gives prayer cards to his orphaned children. (The card shows the icon of Our Lady Mediatrix of all Graces, The Blessed Mother is holding Baby Jesus in the icon) One of the orphaned children prays most devoutly to Our Lady Mediatrix of all Graces, the child told Father that while praying to Our Lady Mediatrix of all Graces, in the church, he felt the heart of Jesus beating on the card. Thump, thump, thump. He prays each night to Our Lady Mediatrix of all Graces icon on the prayer card. It gets very hot to the touch, because the warmth from Father's hands is still there on the card. When the child prays at night and touches the card, he feels Baby Jesus' hand moving. The orphaned child holds the card and feels Baby Jesus' hand moving.

The heat from Father's hands is proof that he is burning up inside. Anything he touches becomes hot.

Padre Pio's blood was also boiling hot because he had the stigmata, his whole interior body was on fire. There's a beautiful movie about Padre Pio and it is recorded at the Vatican, that when Padre Pio first entered the monastery to become a monk, he was intensely sick, and the doctor there examining him kept using thermometers and they kept breaking, going way past the 110 degree mark. And in the movie, it shows the doctor said "I can't believe this, another thermometer broke. I have one last hope". He took out a horse thermometer and used it on Padre Pio, and the horse thermometer, at that point, measured 127 degrees. At 107 degrees we are at the point of death.

Padre Pio's temperature was 127 degrees because his whole body was on fire inside because of the stigmata. I know that because Father David's hands are red hot. When he touches one of our prayer cards, it gets red hot to the touch.

Concerning the gloves of Padre Pio that Father had donated to Francis, he said "Wear white cotton gloves when you hold Padre Pio's gloves. And touch people with the gloves. The smell is beautiful; roses, lilies, lilacs. Very sweet fragrances like fresh roses are coming from the gloves. You can heal yourself with them, Francis. They will work with you because I blessed the gloves many times. I prayed a special prayer for you and your wife. They are going to work for you and you can heal, do the healing yourself. But you have to do it with a lot of faith. Maybe you can heal, I don't know, Francis, maybe you can be an instrument of healing like me. Maybe you are getting a gift. You have to start with the head first; one glove in the left hand and the other in the right hand. You hold them like a Saint Benedict cross. Someone who is contaminated with evil, can give it to you. Holding the gloves in this form will shield you from any evil entering your body. You can't go directly. You say 'In the name of the Father, and of the Son and of the Holy Spirit' and say the person's name. Ask for healing, ask for Padre Pio to pray, to take the evil away from people. Ask for Saint Michael to come and help you and help these people. Ask for Saint Faustina to come and help with this healing. You put the gloves on their heart, then on their back and bring it around and put it on their lungs and then their stomach. Walk around the people with the gloves. When the gloves feel hot, it is healing. It means the people will be healed". I asked if the white cotton gloves are enough insulation (from the heat of Padre Pio's gloves). He said, "Yes."

Before we met, I sent pictures to Father of my beautiful wife Joyce and me and Father said "I saw you in the picture, you look so young. The same way I imagined you, the hair and everything. I imaged how you are looking and the boys. Joyce was the same with her hair long."

Father David has a pacemaker because of the many stresses that he is under running the orphanages for over 500 children; very desolate, sickly children who are in constant need of physical help and hospitalization. He has a lot of volunteers, religious sisters and brothers and a few priests who help him. It's a major responsibility for Father. In addition, he goes out every morning feeding the homeless and searching in the evening for children left on the riverbank to die. So, he has a huge amount of pressure on him. But being the saintly person he is, truly a living saint according to the cardinals, he doesn't ever, ever complain. I never heard him even once say anything, not even harsh words or being tense on the phone.

Father has a pacemaker and has had it for a few years. And sometimes, once a year or so, it has to be adjusted. I don't understand much about pacemakers, but it has to be tweaked. This time it was last November 28th 2013.

He flew into Manhattan, New York. His doctor, at one of the most prestigious hospitals, was the chief surgeon. Father explained this, in our hotel room, after he had recuperated the following day where my wife took the information and was wrote it down. My wife takes very excellent notes.

During surgery, lights flashed from the ceiling, blue lights. (In the operating room there are only white lights, extremely bright white lights concentrated in the middle of the operating room over the operating table) it's always kept very cold there to eliminate the possibility of germs, somewhere perhaps around 50 degrees. It's cold in the operating room, it's a chilling place to be. So Father's in there on, Thanksgiving Day, because the doctor made on exception to see him, being the friend he is to Father David. The operating rooms always have auxiliary lighting. If there is ever a power failure, in the whole entire hospital, the operating room lights will stay on because it has its own generator, which is absolutely necessary when they are operating on someone, that they have the continual flow of lights so that there's no loss of life, they can continue the operation.

It's extremely important to remember and note that when you're in the operating room those lights are constant, they are extremely bright and they are continual, they never, never go out, they never flicker, they never blink. In this case, Father was in the operating room and the lights started flashing. That's a shocking thing for the doctor, who just cut into the patient, to see. Then, there were blue lights around the operating room (there are no such thing as blue lights in the operating room). Blue, of course, is the color of the Virgin Mary. Then, the room filled with the scent of roses. The aroma was so strong that the doctor asked the nurse, "Do you have perfume on?" And the nurse looked very shocked and said "No, doctor". (I believe they are not allowed to wear perfume in the operating room) They all smelled the sweet fragrance of roses – the principle doctor, the doctor assisting, and anesthesiologist, who was also a doctor, and two nurses. All five smelled the very strong sweet fragrance of roses that filled the operating room.

A blue light in the shape of a sphere came down from the ceiling, and like a laser beam, came right directly onto Father's body.

The doctor reported – "The light came down like a scanning machine. A sphere of light came down onto Father. Then it broadened out and scanned Father's body with blue light" - to the shock of the stunned 5 witnesses who reported this. The two surgeons were Jewish, and Father, while under anesthesia was speaking the ancient Aramaic language. Father was speaking to the Blessed Virgin Mary. The reason we know that, is, that after the operation the Jewish doctors said "I know you were speaking ancient Aramaic, I understood much of it because of my Jewish ancestry" I, Francis, have to assume he (Father) was talking to the Blessed Mother as in "The Passion of the Christ" when Mel Gibson in his wisdom, used the ancient Aramaic language. So he (Father) was speaking ancient Aramaic when he was under anesthesia.

The blue sphere of light came down from the ceiling, almost like a broad laser beam, directly onto Father's stomach or body, where the operation was. The next thing that happened was the most startling of all. In this operating room, at a world class hospital, with two surgeons and the anesthesiologist and two nurses, (and they were in their scrubs, masks, hats, gloves, gowns, covered shoes – they scrubbed before dressing, instruments were sterilized). Picture the scene, its immaculate, no germs allowed in the operating room. All of a sudden, the doctor looks and he sees a bearded man in the corner of the room. The other doctor also saw the bearded man. They all saw him in the corner of the room with rosary beads in his hand. Obviously, it was Padre Pio. Father is Padre Pio's "grandson". Padre Pio is his "Nonno". Padre Pio was watching over his grandson in the corner of the operating room, praying the rosary continually, as he always does. The doctor, the chief surgeon, with great alarm said, "Who is that man?! You can't be in here! What are you doing here?! Get out of here!" The doctors, who were in the middle of the surgery, could not leave the patient to rush out and get a security guard, they had to concentrate on continuing the operation of fixing the pacemaker.

The doctors said it was a real person standing there (not a ghost-like image), it was a real bearded man standing in the corner of the operating room with rosary beads in his hand praying the rosary (not in illusion, not a hologram image). After the operation (about an hour later), Padre Pio, the bearded man disappeared - completely vanished before the doctors' absolutely astonished eyes. As soon as Father's pace maker was adjusted and the stitches were finished, the chief surgeon ran to the door and looked down the hallway. Where was this man that was so disruptive? No one was there. He couldn't find, in the hallway near the operating room, anyone there. So again: Father is operated on, the lights flicker, they turn blue, there is the fragrance of roses, there's a blue light all over the entire ceiling, it comes together into a point like a laser beam and goes directly over Father, into him. That was the Blessed Mother being there. Father starts talking in ancient Aramaic and speaking to the Blessed Mother, who was watching over him. Padre Pio then appears in the corner of the room praying the rosary. The doctors are shocked, yelling at the man "Get out of here, what are you doing?" (For sanitary reasons they don't want anything exposed to germs) The man sometime soon after disappears. The operation is over the doctors are shocked. The doctor looks down the hallway and there's no one there.

On the first day of Chanukah, the doctor invited Father to the Chanukah table. The entire family of the doctor was there. Over 24 relatives of the doctor were at his home in Long Island for the feast of Chanukah. Father was an invited guest. I said to Father "You went to Chanukah? You don't speak Hebrew". Father said, "Yes, I do." And he started speaking in Hebrew to me. Father spoke Hebrew at the Chanukah table. (He also speaks Italian, French, German, Spanish, Latin, Croatian and Swahili) I asked Father, "You were there for the Chanukah meal? Did you leave then? Did they bring you back to the hotel?" "No, I stayed four days with the family there and then they brought him back to Manhattan."

When Father came out of the hospital, in November of 2013, we met in the hotel where we were both staying. I brought with me 15 different photographs belonging to Father David. I had our printing company make 20 to 40 copies of each photograph. Father blessed them with the All Powerful Liberating Blessing, then with the Exorcism Blessing, and again he blessed them in Latin.

He sprinkled Holy Water all over the photographs. These are available for purchase to help Father David's orphanage. They come in three sizes, 5x7, 8x10 and 11x14. There are 15 different photographs with the description and number of each photograph under the photo. These are a limited series.

37

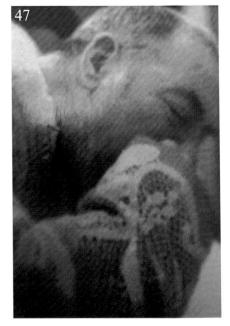

I have asked Father David on different occasions about releasing the picture of Our Lady of Revelations. I again asked Father if we could release the picture of Our Lady of Revelations, standing on the globe with the crescent moon under her feet, with the twelve stars around her head, with the rays pouring out of her palms – the most beautiful flesh-like real image of Blessed Mother. Her gown is very soft but out of focus. He had taken the picture of this. The more than 20 foot high image of Blessed Virgin Mary. I asked him again are we able to release the picture And he said, "No, no, no, no, no, no!" Father was alarmed, "I told you, that Blessed Mother will tell us when we could release the picture to the world". I had asked Father several times about this in the last few months and each time it was "No, no, no, no, no!" We're waiting for Blessed Mother to give permission to release this picture to the world. My personal assumption was it would be released around July 4th, just as the chastisement in the world was occurring. However, I just now learned, within the last week, that Father said (he believes, he doesn't know for sure), but he feels Blessed Mother will allow the release of this picture July 27th. That tells me that if Fathers assumption is correct, the picture of the rays covering all the earth with the rays of grace, like the Lady of the Miraculous Medal, Our Lady Mediatrix of all Graces, pouring grace out of her hands to sooth her children, would be released after, God forbid, the earthquakes, tsunamis, volcanoes and tribulations all over the world that may (I repeat may) come about July 4th to July 27th and beyond.

I again asked Father, two or three weeks ago, if he has seen Blessed Mother recently. He said he saw her last week, she came. It was very brief; maybe three minutes. In the past, Father David had apparitions with Blessed Mother that lasted over a half hour. My assumption is the apparitions last half an hour to 45 minutes or more. But this was very brief, it was only three minutes. She was blessing something and that was it. She did not say anything. "She was very, very quiet you know." I asked Father "is it going to happen, the tribulation, all over the world, earthquakes?" Father said, "It will happen all over the world you know. Earthquakes in California, a lot. Accidents in Chile, Nicaragua.

I asked him if he was coming back to the United States or if he was going to travel, he said Blessed Mother told him not to travel anywhere in June and on. I said, "Father what are you going to be doing?" he said he "would be praying continually all day and all night" for June, July and on. Father said, "I was supposed to go to Rome in May, I cancelled it, I can't go now. They want me there for a meeting". I asked, "Who?" Father said, "The Vatican." I said, "Father, does the Vatican know what's happening, or what may happen?" Father did not respond.

Padre Pio appears to Father David very often. At every healing that he does, Padre Pio guides the gloves, actually their moving on their own, when Father David moves the gloves in the sign of the cross over the body of people on their head, their throat, back, chest, stomach, then they start moving

40

themselves, the gloves start moving automatically and Padre Pio is speaking to Father about what is going on in the body. So Padre Pio is giving Father this information all the time.

I asked, "Did you ask Padre Pio about this?" (meaning the coming chastisements) Father David replied, "When I saw him, he was praying the rosary. He was moving his head, shaking it up and down." Father David had asked Padre Pio, "Is something bad coming?" Padre Pio was shaking his head up and down. "Will evil destruction engulf the whole world?" He (Padre Pio) was shaking his head yes. Father asked it twice and was answered twice with a yes. Father then said, "He was praying the rosary very fast. Faster than before. He was anxious with a worried look on his face. Something more bad is going to be, he was very nervous, I never saw him more nervous. He was different, very, very scared. You can see the face like panic or something. The same thing is happening to me." Father said, then nervously laughed, "I'm worried about it, too". I said "You're worried, too, Father". "I'm worried because the Blessed Virgin said to me 'THE WORLD IS NOT LISTENING TO MY CALL. I'M HOLDING THE HAND OF MY SON'". I said, "Back?" Father David answered, "Yes, she's holding back the hand of her Son back. God is very angry at us you know". I said to Father "What do we tell people?" He said, "Be prepared. Be prepared. Candles in the home. We don't know if there will be a darkness. Cook with charcoal."

On November 7, 2010 Vicka from Medjugorje called Father David from Medjugorje and asked for prayers from him, and also for Masses. Vicka calls Father David very often for his prayers for people. Other renowned priests also ask Father David for his prayers and Masses. *VICKA TOLD FATHER DAVID THAT, "JESUS WAS COMING SOON!"* During that November 7, 2010 phone conversation with Father David "Vicka told Father that something terrible was going to happen in the world on March 11, 2011 in 4 months and she asked for Father David to pray about it! Vicka did not know exactly what was going to happen except that it would be very bad! Father told me about this so we could all pray about this terrible thing that was going to happen. Father also told me that he did not know what it could be. It turned out to be the terrible 9.0 magnitude earthquake - the 5th. most powerful earthquake in history which even set the earth off its axis and which triggered a tsunami 133 feet high ('up to 40 meters high') that traveled 6 miles inland in Japan killing tens of thousands of people! Also, Japan's nuclear power plants were severely damaged resulting in massive radioactive leaks and fallouts and an increase in radiation across Japan and many parts of the world for many months following this massive disaster. It was the most costly disaster in history. *Vicka knew the exact date in advance and told Father the exact date it would occur 4 months before it happened! Again, Vicka also told Father "Jesus was coming!"*

When Father David was in Medjugorje in 1999, and was praying before the 10 foot statue of Our Lady on apparition hill, Jesus appeared to Father in the Divine Mercy rays. The rays were on all four sides of the statue and bathing

Father in the rays. A Franciscan took a photo of Father David praying and the Franciscan reported this to Pope John Paul II. Pope John Paul II then wanted to meet with Father ask about the Divine Mercy experience. Pope John Paul II is the one who brought about Divine Mercy Sunday and veneration to Divine Mercy. The Holy Father asked Father David how the visions of Divine Mercy of Jesus started. How did they appear? Father David said the seven colors of the rainbow (the seven colors are red, yellow, orange, green,blue, indigo, violet) are in the Divine Mercy rays. They covered the ten foot statue. All four sides of the statue were bathed in the seven colors of the rainbow. Pope John Paul II was very amazed.

Father got e-coli bacteria, and was in the hospital three days. Severe stomach pains, colitis and diarrhea for three days. "Padre Pio was always sick, since (he was) 20 years old," says Father David, "I am very similar. Oh, my God, a lot of things that happened to him, are happening to me! Very strange! It's all very strange! We're like twins, they persecuted Padre Pio and persecute me, too. People are very jealous around you when you have gifts. I have the gift of healing, you know. I never knew I had that gift of healing. Padre Pio used to tell me all the time, you have a beautiful gift, but I never asked him what he meant by that. Padre Pio said to me 'Someday you will be a healer like me'. I told him I'll be afraid. Padre Pio said 'Do not be afraid, one day you are going to be like me'. I said which way? He said 'In every way. Little by little you're going to be discovered'. I said to Padre Pio what do you mean? He answered, 'You are going to heal people, you are never going to be contaminated within. You have a special gift from God'. And I discovered my gift. Somebody called me in Naples, Italy, in a monastery, and somebody was dying – a friend of mine – a priest, Marcello. They called me and said Marcello wants to see you, I said why? 'Because he is in intensive care'. So I went to the hospital and there were tubes all over his body in intensive care. I put the gloves of Padre Pio on him, and three days later he was healed". (The reason he said "contaminated" is that Father David was saying, how can I heal, what about diseases and what about the devil when exorcised, and that's what he was getting at.)

"In Paris I was visiting a friend of mine, in Pasteur hospital and someone asked me to please see their son, he is very sick. The boy was from Argentina. I went to the man's son to heal him. I went into the room and the lady said to me 'How did you know in which room was my son?'"

He (the boy) had a sickness from the Amazon. He had malaria. Father said, "I see people coming out with masks, no one told me. Why didn't you tell me, because my (Padre Pio's) gloves are now contaminated with malaria!" The doctor put Father David in isolation. The gloves had to be washed many, many times to clean them (from any risk of transferring malaria). A plane was leaving to go to Argentina (to bring the boy to a hospital there for further treatment). Two doctors came in and said he doesn't have to go, because he is healed. This child was miraculously healed by Father David.

I asked, "Does the Vatican know about these miracles? " "Yes, but they keep it secret, low profile, a lot of priests are persecuted. Vatican knows of stigmata. Only three or four people know about it".

Father David said, "I remember when I went to Pope John Paul II's visitors office, and the scent of roses was very heavy and he said 'What is that?' and I said, that's you Holy Father". The Holy Father has had the Vatican doctor examine Father David's stigmata. The doctor said "This is a very real one, you know".

As a result of the gloves being put through the decontamination process for the extremely deadly and contagious malaria, the gloves shrunk. To this day Father David uses the shrunken gloves of Padre Pio which brought about dozens and dozens of miracles through the last ten years or so since the decontamination. He (Father David) has six pairs of Padre Pio's gloves. But he uses those shrunken gloves because they are irreplaceable - the most precious in the world.

The gloves are the most miraculous gloves of Padre Pio because, quite shockingly, when my wife was touching scapulars (over a 100 scapulars) to the gloves of Padre Pio, very reverently, wearing white cloth gloves when picking up our scapulars and touching them directly to the gloves of Padre Pio, she pointed and said, "What do you think of this?" The gloves had been set down on 9 pages of 32 pound extra thick finest white paper and to my shock there was blood serum that came out of the glove the size of a dime underneath the middle of Padre Pio's blessing hand glove. In the middle of that dime size blood serum, was a pinhead of blood. The blood and the serum soaked through four of the sheets of paper. The red, rich blood was so boiling hot that it bent, warped and curled the paper under it. Just a pinhead of blood in the middle of the serum but it raised the paper up in the air. Several months after the first of the serum appeared, 52 droplets of blood serum came out of the 60 year old gloves of Padre Pio - the blood liquefied in the gloves he wore, it liquefied and dropped onto the white paper underneath. So along with the dime size amount of blood serum, and the pinhead of blood, 52 tiny droplets of blood serum have come out of Padre Pio's most miraculous gloves. You can see some or all of it on our website: www.marysway.net.

When I lifted up the gloves, it looked like a tiny fragment of a rose petal under it. I said to myself, "How did that get there?" I blew on it very gently; it fluttered up in the air. I still didn't understand it. Still holding the glove, I blew on what was about a quarter inch square, that little fragment, which I still felt was a fragment of a rose petal, a deep blood red rose petal, I blew on it again (without touching it) and it fluttered up in the air.

In Padre Pio's case and when he had the stigmata in life, the blood coagulated, stiffened and caked into scabs of blood. Those scabs eventually broke off and a very few people in the world have those scabs. I know a priest that came to the United States and had an actual scab from Padre Pio's hands. There may be only 2 or 3 scabs in the world, which are first class relics.

I realized the tiny fragment under the glove was the scab from Padre Pio that went through 60 or 70 years of time, went across 5000 miles from San Giovanni Rotondo where Padre Pio was, went over the ocean and went under the glove of Padre Pio. That scab of blood was never on the glove, never in the glove of Padre Pio, it just miraculously appeared under the glove.

We touch the religious articles to the scab of blood. So we have the two most miraculous gloves Father gave us. In addition, because of our healing work here, Father David gave me another glove of Padre Pio. We actually have three of Padre Pio's gloves here. The fragrance of roses, lilies and lilacs come pouring out of those gloves. Also, blood serum has come out of that third glove.

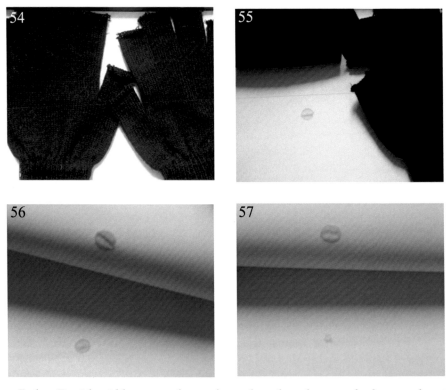

Father David said he wanted us to have them here because he knows about the work we do worldwide for Padre Pio and for the Blessed Virgin Mary.

The three miraculous 12" lifelike statues of Padre Pio are exuding blood and the sweet fragrance of roses, lilies and lilacs, the floral fragrance, the "odor of sanctity" – the same that came out of Saint Padre Pio's hand and wounds, the same that is coming out of Father David's wounds, that same aroma is coming from the statues. The reason the statues are bleeding and exuding the sweet fragrance is because Father blessed them. A few days after Father blessed the first statue, it started bleeding and oiling and having the sweet fragrance.

When Father flew into the United States he donated a second identical statue of Padre Pio and a statue of St. Benedict. When we were in the conference room, we saw it was just a beautiful statue with no blood serum, no oil, nothing coming out of Padre Pio's statue, the same with St. Benedict. Father blessed the statues in front of us. The conference room was locked (only the manager had the key). The next morning we went down, my wife Joyce went in first, we followed. We saw the statue was bleeding and the face was exuding blood. The St. Benedict statue was exuding blood from the head. Father had blessed them, that's the reason they were bleeding.

Father gave a third statue (of Padre Pio) to a woman who was visiting and had the stigmata. The next day he blessed it and she brought it home and it started bleeding.

On Father David's next visit with the devout woman, he brought her a statue of Padre Pio. On their next meeting, in the presence of Francis, the devout woman showed Father and Francis a photograph of her profusely bleeding Padre Pio statue with the mouth turned downward into a frown and sorrowful look. In addition to the bleeding, the statue changed - the face and mouth with the lips turned downward into a sad look.

I asked him to donate another statue of Padre Pio to a benefactor and when he brought the statue down, it was bleeding all over. The sweet fragrance was so strong, blood was pouring out and going onto the pedestal, onto the desktop. So we had to blot it up with tissue and gave it to Father, because we are not allowed to touch that sacred blood. I brought a cylinder flower vase for the occasion of fitting it over the statue and put that approximately 15" flower vase, with very thick glass, over the statue of Padre Pio. And the blood poured through the opening on the bottom. It was pouring out, so I asked Father, "Father, we can't stop the bleeding, the blood is just pouring out all over from your statue that we're giving to the benefactor, is it okay if I use tape, clear tape around the bottom to seal it off?" He said, "Fine." I took a 1" wide clear tape and taped the glass covering to the bottom to the pedestal that the Padre Pio statue was standing on to seal it off completely.

The next day I drove Father to the benefactor's house and explained to her that I had put tape on it (the statue) with Father's permission. Instead of having one other person at her house, the woman had 25 people there. She said to me "Do you mind, this man is finishing a nine day novena, can we have him meet Father?" I said, "Fine, that's okay". So, instead of having the benefactress and her husband and one other person, there were 25 people there looking for healing. Father was surprised, but took two hours to bless the people with the gloves of Padre Pio and performed a healing service.

I explained to the her that the statue was a donation to her for her gift to help the orphanages. Also, that I had to seal off the bottom of the statue's glass covering with tape to keep the blood from oozing out. I asked Father, "Should I leave it that way or should I take the tape off and show the benefactress and the 25 people there?" Father said, "Okay, take the tape off". I carefully, slowly pulled back the tape, lifted the glass up over the statue and the whole room filled with the fragrance of roses, lilies and lilacs. Filled with it! We left

the statue there as a gift. It is the fifth statue that Father blessed that started bleeding. There are pictures of it on our website.

It's been reported by a woman who has known Father for several years, that when Father blesses homes, he blesses the Holy Pictures on the walls and the next day the pictures start oiling. (Father David is no longer able to conduct any further healing services or bless anyone's home, because of the dire times we are approaching).

Father also donated the most precious gift, received by Padre Pio that his family gave him. For Padre Pio's 65th birthday his nieces and nephews and relatives, hand sewed a magnificent stole for Padre Pio to use in the confessional. It was given to Father from Padre Pio's niece, after his death. Padre Pio had willed his personal items to his family and the family gave them to Father David. Father told me he has the stole of Padre Pio and he wore it, but it's very heavy and very long. (Its 9 feet 1 inch long) Father said, "I'm going to donate it to you, Francis, and to Mary's Way, for your good use". The stole is here at Mary's Way to Jesus Worldwide Apostolate. On the inside white neckband of the stole is Padre Pio's blood and sweat from when he was in the confessional 16-18 hours a day. This was his favorite stole. You can see pictures of him with it.

We touch all of our religious articles also to the stole which has his blood and sweat on it. The stole is almost 80 years old now.

Enthralled by the gift icon, Father David placed this icon above the altar in his personal chapel behind the tabernacle. The following day, The Miraculous Icon® miraculously began exuding oil and blood-like serum profusely. Father David put a sterling silver vessel at the bottom of the icon to capture the copious amounts of serum. The miraculous serum has been continuously flowing for over 3 years. Some of the miraculous oil was given by Father to Francis at Mary's Way Apostolate to touch to all the religious items he offers. The miraculous oil from The Miraculous Icon® Father David gave to Francis is multiplying itself!

The Miraculous Icon of Our Lady Mediatrix of All of God's Graces®.

Father David's community provides shelter to homeless orphans. One of the orphans discerned a call to become a priest and received permission from Father David to become a Seminarian for his community. Father David was the only family he had, and his time at the seminary became a very lonely experience. Being brought up in the orphanage, Father always prayed in front of the Our Lady Mediatrix of all Graces Icon with him and the other orphans. Wanting to be reminded of home, the seminarian wanted his mother, the miraculous icon of Our Lady Mediatrix of All of God's Graces.

Father David was touched by this and consented to loan him the icon for a short time; until he acclimates to the Seminary and his distance from Father David.

While the miraculous icon was in the Seminary Chapel on loan to the seminarian in 2012, a different Seminarian was expelled for misbehaving, and in spite, grabbed the miraculous icon off the wall, and left the Seminary with the intent of destroying this precious item of the Seminary community.

Immediately, his hands became blistered, as he left the Seminary grounds. He experienced great burns on his hands which were confirmed by the other Seminarians, and he became terrified. He thought that he would die and go to hell. Being overcome by fear, he brought The Miraculous Icon® back and confessed this sin to a Priest. Father David assumed custody of the Miraculous Icon and refuses to let it out of his sight. Father David prays every day before this image, offering every Mass and every Rosary people request from Father David from Mary's Way Apostolate through the icon of Our Lady Mediatrix of All of God's Graces!

http://www.marysway.net/730-masses-by-stigmata-priest-for-intentions.

60-62

I remember Father telling me that we know, factually, that he has been hospitalized many times in a very similar way that Padre Pio was. I think it was from the age of 20 on, Padre Pio was often sick and had to go home to his family, for example, because he was very sick and had to leave the monastery many years ago. Father also explained to me that one of the times he was hospitalized, he brought the gloves with him for healing purp[?] patients in the hospital. When he was being examined by the doctor[?] couple of days stay for his own work, he took the gloves and hid the[?] his pillowcase of his bed so that no one would take them. It was a good an[?] wise precaution because the sweet fragrance of roses, lilies, and lilacs were coming from the gloves and it was detected by a person who visited his room and actually stole the gloves. He saw Padre Pio's gloves, pulled them out of the pillowcase and stole the gloves. It was eventually reported back to Father that the person who had Padre Pio's gloves had tried to use them for healing purposes and they did not work, obviously, because they were taken from Father's pillowcase. Therefore, one of the pairs of gloves was missing. Father no longer brings the gloves when he has to have a hospital stay because the sweet fragrance emanates and there is no place to put them safely.

When Father was in the private audience with Pope John Paul II in 1999, Holy Father again asked him to explain all about the Divine Mercy. There were no pictures taken during that private audience. It was very private. This is all from Father David's reporting to me. In the room was a Monsignor, a Cardinal, and Father David. They went up the private elevator. What that tells me, because I am familiar with the Vatican, is that they went up the elevator to Pope John Paul II's private residence. On the first floor are the public offices of the Vatican. The second floor holds the administrative offices of the Pope. The third floor includes his private office and private library. There are very beautiful massive rooms adorned with original artwork by Rafael, Botticelli, and other renaissance masters, which I passed through on my way to my private audience with Pope John Paul II when he blessed the Miraculous Icon. The third floor is where he gives his Apostolic Blessing out the window at Easter, Christmas, and such times as that. That is when we see the Pope in front of 300,000 people at Saint Peter's Square. That is how many people Saint Peter's Square holds. The fourth floor (the Pope's residence) is only accessible by the elevator and that elevator comes from the ground floor in Saint Peter's Basilica next to the Pieta with a sealed off room and chamber. So when Father said they went up a private elevator, that is what happened. Father also told us that he had come back in 2002 for another private audience with Pope John Paul II. The reason it was a private visit with just the Cardinal, Monsignor, and Pope John Paul II and Father David is that the Vatican wants to keep Father David's identity confidential.

The scapulars that I had given to Father David, he had given to a priest that was in charge of the hospital he had been in. The priest said, "I feel very good; very secure." It was because of the scapular. "He has a lot of respect for me", Father David said. And the priest said, "Bless me Father." So the priest in charge of the hospital had asked for Father David's blessing. This priest who was in charge of the entire hospital was asking for Father David's blessing. There was also a doctor in the hospital who Father had prayed over as well.

Father had a bad dream about fires in the Middle East. I asked him, "Is it

'The fires in the Middle East will be very soon." It was a
,ut turmoil in the Middle East.

,or said to Father David in an apparition, "All the prophecies
, year, but it is not too late to stop it." That is extremely
be mitigated or lessened. Blessed Mother can continue to
n of Jesus from striking us for our bad behavior.

Father mentioned about the Saint Benedict medals that are blessed by the
Benedictines in Italy. They bless them while making them from the molds
from the inside out. Then they are sent to Father's monastery and they are
left on his Altar for 9 days where there are 18 masses; a Latin Mass in the
morning and an evening Gregorian Mass. So there are 2 masses every day for
9 days. The medals are right there on the side of the altar which Father blesses
with holy water and incense and a liberating blessing along with an exorcism
blessing which is very powerful. He said what to do with the medals is to put
them in the middle of windows or on the edges of windows. Have the cross
facing outside with Saint Benedict facing you. This is very important. Tape it
there. You have the most powerful protection. You do the same on the door
even though it is solid; you still have the same protection. You also put it on
the four corners on the inside of your home. Rooms where you sleep should
have medals also. Father said to go outside your home and dig a hole in the
four corners of your home and place a medal in each hole. This will protect
your home from earthquakes. It will also protect your gas lines and water
lines from breaking. So you will have it on the inside and outside of your
home. You will have 8 Saint Benedict medals for your home. He said to get
holy water. You can even get a gallon of bottled water and go to your pastor
or priest and asked them to bless this water. Mark the gallon as holy water.
This way you can keep it for tumultuous times if you need. Get alter incense
for your home and put a cross outside with Jesus facing the street so you will
have that protection. A Saint Benedict cross protects against intruders. Even a
regularly blessed cross will protect you from intruders. No harm will come to
you. Evil will stay away. Enemies will stay away. Always carry with you the
Saint Benedict cross and don't let anyone touch it. The reason is you do not
want it contaminated. It is very important to keep it close to your heart and
pure. Keep it in the open don't let anyone touch it.

These most powerfully blessed Saint Benedict medals with the all powerful
"Liberating Blessings" are offered by Mary's Way. Father David, the miracle-
working priest which Pope John Paul II witnessed and confirmed his Stigmata
wounds, directly linked to Padre Pio, who is known by the highest ranking
Cardinals in Rome as a "living saint", has provided these most protecting
Saint Benedict medals especially for the 3 days of darkness and chastisement!

Mary's Way offers these medals from Father David to raise funds for
over 500 abandoned and severely disabled children in his orphanages and
extra blessings for you. These medals are very specially made and blessed

to protect and prepare you and your family for the very likely and very possible, soon 3 DAY OF DARKNESS, ENLIGHTENMENT, AND POSSIBLE CHASTISEMENT!

Father David said" "The medals I give you are for protection". He also said: "I bless the medals individually with the all powerful 'LIBERATING BLESSINGS! – which are bigger, stronger blessings than any other blessing!

At the Benedictine Monastery in Italy where the medals are made, the Monks pray continually when making the medals – from the inside out! The Benedictines also pray and bless the medals with the powerful Benedictine Blessing when the medals are finished. The medals are sent to and all reverently placed on my altar in my chapel – where Padre Pio appeared to me praying with Jesus on the Cross.

My Capuchin priests and I pray every day over the medals at the end of Mass for 9 days. We also pray over the medals for 2 hours every night for 9 nights! The medals are blessed in Latin with Holy Water and with Incense. I also bless the medals with "Exorcism Blessings". (Father was trained by the Vatican's Chief Exorcist!)

Always carry or wear your medals and tape them on the inside of every entrance door! Medals should also be taped on the inside four corners of your home and clear-taped to as many windows as possible. The Saint Benedict medals must have Saint Benedict facing you. The Cross faces outward.

Father David said, "These most protective Saint Benedict medals with the most powerful 'Liberating Blessing' protects you, your family, and your home from these 15 disasters: fire, floods, earthquakes, tornadoes, robberies, crime, diseases, epidemics, illnesses, chemical warfare, plagues, poisoning, possession, witchcraft, demons." The medals are quality Italian gold or silver plated 3/4 " in diameter, 1/16" thick and weight .5 ounces. They are available online at www.marysway.net.

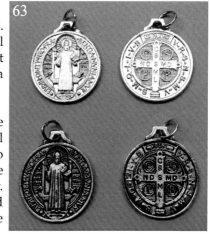

Wear a red wool cord on your left hand. Father gave my family and I red wool cords to wear around our waists that we wear at times when we need extra protection.

When Father was in the hospital he brought the Our Lady Mediatrix of All God's Graces with him in a frame into the room with the cardiologist. When he left that room there appeared a rainbow. So many visitors, including doctors and nurses came up to the room to see the rainbow in the room Father was in, they had to seal off that room because too many people were visiting the room. This has happened before with Father after he has left a room.

Father had a private audience with Pope Benedict. I asked Father, "What was he like?" He said, "Pope Benedict was very quiet, very, very observant. " He was with Pope Benedict on World Youth Day in Barcelona.

Father mentioned that as part of the tribulation, the chastisement, that there will be many earthquakes all over the world. He mentioned several countries Uruguay, Chile, Malaysia, Singapore, Guam, Indonesia. There were earthquakes even in Mexico and Los Angeles as well. He said, "Everywhere now it is starting." I asked Father David about California if there was a big one coming. He said, "Yes, yes."

I had asked Father David about Padre Pio's blood type. He said he had inquired and found out about Padre Pio's blood type. Padre Pio was beaten by the devil and there was blood all over the bed, the pillowcases, the sheets, and all over. Most interesting is that Padre Pio's blood type is AB positive which is the same as the blood type as on the Shroud of Turin and the Eucharistic Miracle. Jesus' blood was AB positive. That has been confirmed. Father David has the same blood type as Saint Padre Pio and Jesus Christ! This is very interesting information. Father has the stigmata and Saint Padre Pio had the stigmata.

Padre Pio prayed to Our Lady Mediatrix of All Graces for 50 years and that is common information. Padre Pio would always tell people when they came to thank him for the prayers, the miracles, and healings "Don't thank me. Thank Our Lady Mediatrix of All Graces, because she is the one which all the

graces come through from Jesus. She is the one that distributes all the graces." Father David said, "That's why we met. So many people in the world, and we met. Amazing! God put everything together."

The question I asked Father David was how many times Jesus has appeared to him in the Divine Mercy. He said, "Jesus and the Divine Mercy appeared to me many times. Sister Faustina also appeared to me in 1982."

CHAPTER 5
Does the Devil Really Exist?

A great number of people in the world do not believe there is a devil. They question if the devil really exists. Is there proof that the devil exists? Aside from the evil that is in the world or great evil depending on how you look at it, what other proof is there that the devil really exists. Has anyone ever taken a picture of the devil to prove that he really exists?

Through the grace of God and through the graces of "Our Lady Mediatrix of All Graces," we have an actual photograph of the evil one (the devil) which Father David exorcised from a group of 50 people about 5 years ago. This most astonishing actual photograph first shows the Blessed Mother in an extremely bright glowing light over the 50 people, protecting everyone from the devil that Father David exorcised from the people that he was praying over! This is one of the most striking photographs Father David has ever given to me. This picture was taken while Father David was performing a healing service exorcism in the evening outdoors. When the picture was developed, and they gave it to Father David, two extremely striking things were found in the photograph – one is very noticeable and the other is not.

One is the brilliant white hot silhouette of Blessed Mother in the air hovering over all the people with her rays of graces coming out of her in all directions, onto all the people, protecting them in this evening prayer service. Emanating from Blessed Mother are blessings and graces in the form of rays almost like tongues of fire coming out of her body showering onto all the people. It is a magnificent photograph! But the most striking thing in the photograph is that while Father was praying over them, and exorcising them, *you can see his hand in the left side of the photo casting out their demons, you can also actually see the devil's huge head which was decapitated in Father David's exorcism in the lower right corner, with fire in his slanted eyes, going back into hell, upside down!* You will just see his massive burned, blackened head, nose, mouth, and what looks like folded bat like wings close to the head! The devil is upside down going back into hell where he belongs!

Father David literally exorcised the devil from the people, and for the first time ever, you can actual see a photograph of THE EVIL ONE – BEING TOSSED BACK INTO HELL!

But fear not. Blessed Mother is there protecting us with her blessing, and her rays of graces pouring out all over. Blessed Mother's rays of grace, are covering and tossing the evil one back into hell upside down. IT IS THE DEFINITIVE ULTIMATE PROOF THAT THE DEVIL EXISTS!

A second extremely striking example occurred to me about 17 years ago when a priest appeared to me in a dream, he was very tall and thin with a narrow face and long nose. He had a kind of large white crossed-over bib around his neck in place of the modern-day collar which priests wear today. It was old and of French design. It was about 200 years old. This priest was walking down an aisle in the church that I usually attend. I was sitting off to the right side of the pews. The priest came down from the altar after that Mass and was walking down the long aisle coming directly at me. This is in a dream. I remember vividly, exactly, everything this priest said to me. I wrote down his exact words shortly after it happened. His exact words to me were: "Because of your dedication, diligence, and devotion you will be receiving a Sacred Icon of the Blessed Virgin Mary! It will be like a relic of the Blessed Virgin Mary, a life-like real image of the blessed Virgin Mary!"

The next morning when I woke up I was in seventh heaven. I was the happiest I ever was in my life! I was going to get an actual image and Icon, a life-like image of the Blessed Virgin Mary! It was going to be like a sacred relic of her. But when I woke up I realized there were no such images or relics of the Blessed Virgin Mary anywhere, so I dismissed it as it was just a dream. I was, however, still extremely happy about the dream. The priest in the dream intrigued me. I wondered who the priest in the dream was. I remember seeing Mother Angelica live television programs which I have been watching for 30 years. I thought it must have been a priest in one of Mother Angelica's EWTN television network series. But that priest wore glasses. This one in the dream did not wear glasses. They both were tall and had narrow faces, but two things were striking in the dream. The priest did not have glasses and he had this old habit.

So I dismissed it. But I was still intrigued by this. Who was the century's old priest who was the messenger of Blessed Mother who relayed this message to me? I have hundreds of religious books in my personal library. I have many picture books of Saints. I went through every one looking for that particular face of the priest which I felt was a saint. I went to numerous libraries even distant ones and went through hundreds of picture books of Saints looking for that priest in the dream. It actually occurred on the 15th anniversary of Medjugorje, June 24, 1996 I was noting the date that it occurred. Still trying to puzzle through what it was all about, wondering would I ever receive this magnificent image of the Blessed Virgin Mary. Finally five weeks later, on a Saturday, the day devoted to the Blessed Virgin Mary. I found the picture of the saint in one of the books. I was shocked. It was Saint Louis de Montfort the most Marian of all saints! I rushed home. I told my wife that it was Saint Louis de Montfort, who appeared to me in the dream, which gave it more validity. More importantly, I found it on July 26th, the feast day of Saint Anne and Saint Joachim, the mother and father of Blessed Mother and the grandmother and grandfather of Jesus. This was a further sign to me that Blessed Mother had arranged this; the Mother and Father of Blessed Mother and the Grandmother and Grandfather of Jesus.

The second part of the dream occurred on the Feast of The Holy Rosary, October 7th.. Proving how powerful the Blessed Mother is the devil appeared to me in a dream. He looked exactly the same as the picture of the devil that Father David exorcised from the people. He had the same burned, blackened, massive head; the same big wide, huge nose, and the same mouth which is much bigger than a grizzly bear or a gorilla. He was massive; over 8 feet tall and probably weighed well over 1,000 pounds.

When he attacked me in the dream, I was extremely horrified. I yelled out "Mother, Mother, help me, help me, save me!" And in a millisecond the devil was gone! But the devil never gives up. So in a matter of minutes he came back at me again and again. I again yelled "Mother, Mother, help me, help me, save me, save me" and again in a millisecond he was gone! He came back at me a third time, a fourth, a fifth, and a sixth time. The devil never gives up. And each time I cried out for Our Blessed Mother to help me. And each time, in a millisecond he was gone! This proves how instantly the evil one flees from the name of Mary, and how extremely powerful the Blessed Virgin Mary is over the devil! The point I am trying to make is the exact same image I saw 17 years ago was exactly the same as the image in the photograph taken at Father David's healing service 5 years ago.

Have no fear. Our Blessed Mother protects us!. Just pray to Saint Michael the Archangel when being attacked, and cry out for Blessed Mother to help you – and the evil one will flee!

CHAPTER 6

December 2013 Revelation
What you need to know to survive the Chastisement

Matthew 13:24-30 "He put before them another parable: 'The kingdom of heaven may be compared to a man who sowed good seed in his field; but while everybody was asleep, an enemy came and sowed weeds among the wheat, and then went away. So when the plants came up and bore grain, then the weeds appeared as well. And the servants of the house came to the man and said; 'Master, did you not sow good seed in your field? Where, then, did these weeds come from?' He answered, 'An enemy has done this.' And the servants said to him, 'Then do you want us to go and gather them?' But he replied, 'No, for in gathering the weeds you would uproot the wheat along with them. Let both of them grow together until harvest: and at harvest time I will tell the reapers, collect the weeds first and bind them in bundles to be burned, but gather the wheat into my barn'". I interpret this to mean that evil must co-exist with good. And only at judgment time will they be separated. The point is, judgment day is coming, that is certain. It is likely to happen very very soon according to the apparition that Father David had of the Blessed Mother. THEREFORE, DO NOT JUDGE ANYONE! PRAY FOR EVERYONE! Because we will be held accountable very soon for our condemning people. We ourselves will be held accountable for not praying for those who most need our prayers. As we pray after each decade of the rosary - "Oh, my Jesus, forgive us our sins, save us from the fires of hell, lead all souls to heaven, especially those most in need of thy mercy" Lets pray for everyone in the world, bad and good, to punish the evil one for his transgressions against good people, pray that no one goes to hell. As in the movie "The Passion of the Christ", when Jesus died and was resurrected, we saw very vividly the devil, in what was represented as hell, screaming in a rage because at that point those who were destined to go to hell, through the suffering of Jesus Christ for our sins, were able to go to heaven. In the Our Father, when we pray, we implore God to "forgive us our trespasses, as we forgive those who trespass against us... !"

Blessed Mother appeared to Father December 20 about 3 to 4 months ago. She gave Father dire messages. It was so out of the ordinary that Father David called during the day; around noon time, my time here. He never calls during the day. He is usually busy doing things for the orphanages and so on. I was in the storeroom doing some work out there and he called maybe around 11am and I said "Hold on Father. Let me go to my office. Do you want me to call you back?" I don't want him to be paying for the call. He said, "No, no. That is ok. I will hold on." That was a clue to me that he was not in a hurry or he doesn't mind paying the cost of an international phone call. I told him it would take me a few minutes to get to my office phone, but he said that was fine.

My wife was not home. She was at the post office. I went to my office, shut the door, and each time telling Father I would be right with him. When I got to my office he spoke to me and told me about the revelation the Blessed Mother gave to him. And it was about five minutes long; a very dire message. He was extremely serious. I have listened to him for about four years. This was different. It was very serious. He went directly into the information. He spoke to me about Blessed Mother appearing and giving this message. Now, it was so dire, so incredible. So I said, "Ok Father. I will call you back in the evening', which is what I always do. When my wife gets back we usually call him back together. He gave me a time frame of about six hours later in the evening. .I take very careful accurate written notes about what Father says. It sounded like Father had been crying. Now he is the good Father like the Blessed Mother and does not want to scare her children. Like any mother or father they don't want to scare their children so they hold back on things and don't tell them the worst case scenario. Father is the same way. He doesn't want to scare me or anyone. We are the closest, Father and I and my wife Joyce are the closest associates. There are others, too. Because of the intimate work we do for the Blessed Mother we are very close It really shook me that Father was crying. I said, "Holy Cow. This is the most unique, different message he has ever given me." So now I had a platform to talk to him, so when I called him that night I used that information and in the second or third sentence I asked him, "Father, did you cry on the phone?" There was a pause. I don't know if I repeated it then, but he said, "Yes. I was crying on the phone." He said, "People don't listen. They just don't want to listen." So he was crying because we brought this on ourselves.

Now, the message was very dire. He said explicitly in the first five minute conversation, "Blessed Mother said to tell everyone." You see, that's the Blessed Mother speaking. She is giving Father a direct order. She says, "Tell everyone." She gave the dates. She said the tribulation is going to start in many parts of the world July 4th to the 27th and beyond.. No dates are ever given in any apparition. I have studied every Mary apparition. There is never, ever a date, number one. Number two, Blessed Mother gave explicit direct instructions, very simple and she put it in a way that everyone can understand. She said, "At this point most people are not going to go to heaven." And when you say that, they are going to die; a lot of people are going to die. She didn't say it like that, but I am reading into it. Then she did something that was shocking. She said, "To get into heaven you have to…" She mentioned four things. She said, "Pray the rosary every day. Most people are level two." Now she put it into the vernacular. Level one, level two. Everyone knows levels. She put it so everyone in the whole world could understand. All cultures can understand what levels are. She said, "Most people are level two." All she said was most, so that is the majority of people. Most people are at level two. They are not going to get into heaven. To get into heaven she said, "You have to be a level five." She made it very simple. You go from a two to a five. Father said, "To get to a five, like Blessed Mother said you can get there very quickly, which is the best thing. It does not take years, months, or weeks. Get your act together and within one week you can get to a level five. You can do it real fast". The Blessed Mother did not put it that way, but that is the way the conversation went. The way to get to level five you have to

1). Pray the rosary every day without fail. If you miss two days, then pray three rosaries the next day. Keep records. You have your bank accounts with money in and money out, expenses. Well, why not have a spiritual bank account. Pray so many rosaries a day, say so many Angelus', pray to the Divine Mercy every day. Just write things down. Keep track. The point is just to write it down somewhere. Pray the rosary every day without fail.

2). Confession once a week without fail. Saint Pope John Paul II went to confession every day according to a cardinal from Rome who was on a show on the Eternal Word Television Network. To go to confession means you have sins. If Pope John Paul II went to confession every day, who are we to say, "I don't have any sins. I don't have to go to confession." That's already a sin, the sin of pride. You are already committing another sin. You did commit sins by your pride; by saying you don't have any sins. Whether you know it or not, that's your sin. Confess that next time. So go to confession every week.

3). Do not judge anyone because the judgment is coming. Don't judge anyone whatsoever. Father was emphatic about this. Don't judge anybody. Turn off the televisions; turn off the radios; save your souls and then save the souls of your children and your family by telling them what needs to be done according to the Blessed Mother. First save yourself - like a mother on an airplane putting the oxygen mask on herself first before putting on the infant next to her because she has to make sure she doesn't panic and does it correctly. She saves her soul. Now she is ok and she can take care of the children next to her by putting on their oxygen masks when something happens in an airplane. Save yourself first, then your children and family. Give them this information; tell them about it, start evangelizing.

4). Receive communion every day. Going to mass every day is one thing, but that is not what the Blessed Mother said. She said to receive communion every day. In my opinion, if you cannot go to Mass, making a spiritual communion should suffice.

To sum it all up: 1. Pray the rosary every day. 2. Confession once a week, 3. Don't judge anyone. 4. Receive communion every day. Don't judge anyone is the hardest because that is the hardest to do. In the Our Father we pray "Forgive us our trespasses, as we forgive those who trespass against us." We are annoyed at the person who cut us off on the street. "I'll get you. I'll come and cut you off." That is not forgiving. That is a sin. That is not forgiving others of their trespasses. We have to be careful not to judge anyone, no matter what. Pray for everyone to get into heaven. Pray that everyone goes to heaven; everybody living and dead. Pray they all go to heaven so that hell is empty and that would really tick the devil off. He has no one down there. Pray repeatedly, "Oh My Jesus, forgive us our sins, save us from the fires of hell, lead all souls to heaven, especially those most in need of Thy Mercy". The point is, don't judge anyone. Just pray that everyone goes to heaven. Pray for yourself first, then family, and then everyone else. If you do all four of these things, the Blessed Mother said you will go right to a level 5. Now, I think the way it works is if you do that in one day,; pray the rosary that day, went to confession that week, received communion that day, and did not judge anyone then you are at a level 5 and if you were to die, you would go to heaven. If the next day, you missed the rosary, then you are no longer a level five and if you die you will not go to heaven. Sorry, you are not getting in. That is a very interesting thing. You could die any second. You see people dying all the time. You never know.

The Blessed Mother told Father to tell everyone. Father is a Capuchin Monk and he is in a monastery. He takes care of orphans in orphanages. He has priestly information. He has lots of people who look to him for healings, graces, and masses that he says through us and so on. He has an extremely busy work day. He gets up at six in the morning. When I call him at night it is 9:30 or 10:00 pm and he is just getting ready to sleep. He gets about six or seven hours of sleep. Blessed Mother told him, "Father I want you to tell everybody." He can't. She knows that. Blessed Mother knows he can't tell everybody, but she tells him to tell everybody. Father says, "I don't even have a computer". But if Father can't do this and the Blessed Mother knows he can't do it and Father knows he can't do it, what does he do? He gets up. The Blessed Mother just appeared. He calls me approximately 10:30 in the morning and tells me to tell everybody. He tells me the Blessed Mother says "to tell everybody". Father knows that it is me. Now I have to get out there and tell everybody. I'm the one with the network here, the computers, and the savvy to hire people to get this word out. So now I have to get the word out. Now it is my obligation to do this. If I don't do this, then I am going to be chastised. I have to do it. I have been toying along, figuring out how to do this and trying it myself.

I have put in this book that Blessed Mother has many times before in many apparitions, probably dozens of times, possibly thirty or forty times, said she was holding back her Son's hand - meaning that the chastisement, the punishment and judgment is being held back because the Blessed Mother is holding back her Son's hand. This has been on-going for decades.

Father has said, "Get a lot of holy water, sprinkle it often - every week. Be prepared with blessed salt. Be prepared with blessed 100% beeswax altar candles. Get your wooden matches blessed so you can light the blessed candles for the three days of darkness. Be prepared for 72 hours of darkness, no light, no gases, no nothing. Be prepared." Father continued, "Houses have to be filled with Saint Benedict medals: all houses must have Saint Benedict Medals on all their entrance and exit doors, on all the windows, and in the 4 corners of their homes inside and outside. Tape the medals inside your house on the doors and windows with Saint Benedict facing you. If you have pets place these medals around the necks of pets and on top of birdcages. Place Saint Benedict Medals in the ground (about an inch down) in the four corners of your homes to protect against earthquakes. This will protect people from the demons that are and will be roaming the earth in very great numbers very soon."

Father David told me since Blessed Mother's December 20th 2013 message to him about the chastisement coming very soon: that he now has his special Saint Benedict Medals on every door, and on every window, and in every corner of every room in his monastery! Also, all around the outside of his monastery. You can get these special Saint Benedict Medals that Father David sent to us for your protection from Mary's Way Worldwide Apostolate. For your convenience you can purchase these blessed medals at http://www. marysway.net/saint-benedict-medals/ We have ten thousand Saint Benedict medals here, I expect that quantity will be exhausted quickly, because I cannot get anymore.

Father said: "Lock your doors. When the three days of darkness comes, don't look outside! Don't answer the door! Voices will be similar to what you know. Don't open the door! Get charcoal to cook with, extra food, extra water. Get dark covers for all your windows to be ready for when the 3 days of darkness comes - so you cannot look out and so the evil demons cannot look in." Blessed Mother told Father David there will be lots of evil in the streets everywhere in the world. Don't open the doors to anything. From July 4th through the 27th you may see the letters "M I R" (which means "peace") all over the world in the sky and cloud formations. There will be images of Blessed Mother in the sky all over the world. Whichever image of the Blessed Mother people offer their prayers though, that's the image people will see. A couple hundred different images of Blessed Mother. For example, Our Lady of Fatima, Our Lady of Guadalupe, Our Lady of Lourdes or Our Lady of Czestochowa that is the image that will appear in the sky to that particular person. After the images of Blessed Mother in the sky for seven days, there will appear the sign of the cross in the sky for seven days over the world. Then Jesus' image will also be in the sky.

"Be constantly praying," Blessed Mother told Vicka. "Very bad earthquakes are going to happen - very, very bad" Blessed Mother also said, "Do not be afraid! I will remain with you. Pray the rosary and the Saint Michael prayer continually for three days. Lots of evil will be in the streets! Everywhere in the world!"

Father said: "Do not look outside your windows; you will die of a heart attack! You will be depressed seeing all the demons if you look. Don't open the door to anything. When evil attacks pray 'The Saint Michael Prayer' 20 times in a row:

'Saint Michael the Archangel, defend us in battle, be our protection against

the wickedness and snares of the devil. May God rebuke him, we humbly we pray, and do thou, O Prince of the Heavenly Host, by the power of God, cast back into hell Satan and all evil spirits who roam the world seeking the ruin of souls. Amen!

This prayer is very powerful! Get wooden matches and get them blessed; have plenty of drinking water. Blessed Mother is going to protect us, don't worry."

Then Father said, "There is going to be a lot of wars and a lot of fighting all over the world! For your protection, wear the All Protecting 12-Way Brown Scapulars all the time, that Blessed Mother held out in her hands. This will help people, help a lot. It will bring you a lot of graces". *IN HIS APPARITION WITH BLESSED MOTHER TO FATHER DAVID, BLESSED MOTHER SAID: "WHOEVER WEARS THE SCAPULAR WILL BE PROTECTED! WHOEVER WEARS THE SCAPULAR WILL BE SAVED!"* You can get them from Mary's Way To Jesus Worldwide Apostolate at http://www.marysway.net/12-way-all-protecting-double-scapulars-and-medals/.

People don't pray for souls in purgatory, "Help me get out!", this is the plea from the souls in purgatory.

Father saw the souls in purgatory. "Get me out of here!", they were crying out.

Trumpets of angels are being heard recently. It was reported in the news that strange sounds are being heard in the sky. Jesuits hear it, also. Father David heard the four trumpets of angels. Father told me he had seen the baby angels hiding in the trees. He could see through them. Each trumpet an angel has plays a tune, but when they play all together it's a sad sound.

Father David said, "This is the beginning Francis, they don't know, they don't know. If you don't pray you won't be saved. The gates of hell will be opened all over the world. Time is close, time is close. Something bad, something bad's coming, something very bad in the world".

The priest who has been seeing Blessed Mother said, "It's very sad, because of what is happening all over the world. There is going to come another war, a very bad war. A lot of earthquakes are going to be happening, a lot of disasters in the world. Like tsunamis, earthquakes. People don't pray. This is very very bad. We need to pray and pray and pray".

Father said, "Blessed Virgin Mary never gives dates, now she gives dates. Time is close. Blessed Virgin Mary will appear a lot."

July 4th to July 27th and after, "The doors and walls of Paradise will be open. The gates of hell will be open. Tell everybody Blessed Mother told me, 'Tell the people to be prepared. Rosary, Mass, confession. Judgment coming in July. Do not find fault in anyone. Three days of darkness may be after that. People do not care. They don't know, they don't know. Pray the rosary every day, communion every day, they will be saved. Gates of hell will be opened all over the world. People will be dying. Doors of Paradise will be open also'".

"Doors of purgatory will be opened. You will see signs in the sky (MIR in red) three days of judgment and darkness. Some people will see things happening in the next months. Scary, scary things happening".

"Paradise doors open, you may be able to see your family, those relatives in heaven.(Father had said you must be at a certain level of holiness for this to happen) We are close, Francis, very close. Pray, pray, pray until July. Blessed candles, Holy Water, food for storage, darkness, no sun. This time very bad, very very bad".

"To be good, don't commit sins, don't judge people, don't criticize. Change your life. Blessed Mother is giving the opportunity to change. People don't want to listen, they don't want to change."
Blessed Mother appears more and more often to Father David. "People are not listening, pray, pray, pray, pray, if they want to be safe. St. Benedict medals on the windows the doors, everywhere. Beeswax candles, food storage. Darkness and no sun. Very bad Francis, this time very bad".

"Good, good people nothing will happen to them, very bad people have very little time left to correct their life".

"After that Jesus Christ coming to earth." I, Francis Slinsky, interpret that as the second coming of Jesus.

When I asked Father, "Were you crying, Father?", he said, "Yes, because people don't care. People have time for tv, time for friends, time for computers, time for movies, but time for Blessed Mother? Why don't you pray a lot of Hail Marys, Our Fathers, Glory Be's. People don't have time to pray, the rosary takes ten minutes, you don't have ten minutes?"

I asked, "When people see the Blessed Mother will they be able to take pictures?" Father answered, "Yes". I asked, "Can they touch her", he said, "No, after this comes Jesus Christ back to earth". (As mentioned before Father said you must be at a certain level of holiness to see Blessed Mother.)

CHAPTER 7
What the Bible and other sources have to say about
Revelations and the Apocalypse
Angel Trumpets?

There is an external proof of the possible revelations apocalypse coming because it has been reported in 40 to 50 countries that sounds, very eerie death like sounds of the extremely low resonating pitches are being heard We searched the media. We saw YouTube's. We calculate millions of people have heard and experienced it. This is one of the reasons many reputable news stations around the world have broadcast information about this. Given the fact that some of those news and radio stations have had four hour sessions dedicated to this, it brings the people who have heard this to hundreds of millions.

Father David heard these sounds before anyone in the world. He reported to me that he was looking for land in a beautiful wooded area for an expansion of his orphanage. While he was out there he heard four beautiful trumpet sounds. He didn't understand it. He was there with his brother priests, monks, and seminarians and they all heard it. Father David described it as the angels blowing the trumpets and he felt perhaps that this was the land that the Blessed Mother wanted him to purchase. That is his earliest recollection of hearing these trumpets. In Revelations, there are seven trumpets. When the seventh trumpet sounds, the entire world will be destroyed. So now, we have heard four trumpets. This may be a wake-up call or a dire sign that revelations or could come about soon. Here are some websites that you can listen to (see list that follows) No one has come forth with a complete explanation. They do not understand it because they have not gotten the information from this book. This book is putting together what this is all about. It is my personal belief that it is the angels from Revelations that are blowing the trumpets of warnings and no one is heeding the warning because they do not understand it.

Since the summer of the year 2011 there have been increased reports of "strange sounds" from or in the sky. The following is a list of countries that the sounds have been heard in (many have cell phone or camera recordings of the "sounds" – some even being recorded in August of 2011 at a Tampa Bay's baseball game). United States, England, New Zealand, Brazil, Netherlands, Finland, Romania, Canada, Austria, Czech Republic, Germany, Ireland, Belgium, Spain, Helsinki, Australia, Poland, Greece, Mexico, Hungary, Costa Rica, Sweden, France, Norway, Argentina, Russia, Denmark, Chile, and Ukraine.

While there will always be some hoax videos posted to the internet, but there have been enough people reporting this for several news shows to **cover this** phenomenon.

While many explanations have been offered for the reason for the sounds, (Fracking, volcanoes, earthquakes, space quakes or HAARP - the High Frequency Active Auroral Research Program located in Alaska that uses very low frequency radio waves in its research) which are described as low rumblings, or a low hum, none seem to be a sufficient explanation.

Could these sounds be the "trumpets" of the angels as described in the Book of Revelation in the bible. Rev. 8:6" And the seven angels who had the seven trumpets prepared themselves to sound them".

In the Bible, (Joshua 6), the story of the destruction of the walls of the city of Jericho is told. Men blowing trumpets and marching around the city for seven days. Then at the shout of the people the walls finally fall.

Could the blowing of the trumpets have created strong enough vibrations to have damaged the integrity of the walls around the city? And if so, then what could the sound and vibrations of the trumpets of angels do on the earth?

See "Strange Sounds Around the World" by TrueRealityORG on YouTube
www.Strangesounds.org
http://thefw.com/videos-of-strange-sounds/
www.wn.com
www. Theweeklyconstitutional.com
google – "strange sounds in the sky" and "angel trumpets being heard"

The word Apocalypse means the revelations Saint John the Apostle received from God regarding the future events connected with the end of time.

The following excerpts are from:
Alfred McBride, O. Praem., **The Second Coming of Jesus, Chapter 6,**
The Four Horsemen Are Coming, *(pp. 53-58)*
Copyright © 1993 by Our Sunday Visitor Publishing Division, Our Sunday Visitor, Inc. Scripture texts taken from **The New American Bible With Revised New Testament,** © 1986 Confraternity of Christian Doctrine; **and The Holy Bible, Revised Standard Version,** © 1946 Division of Christian Education of the National Council of Churches of Christ in the United States of America.

Who's in Charge?

In a bloody battle scene in Francis Ford Coppola's film, Apocalypse Now, a messenger wanders into the front lines. Dazed by the chaos, he asks, "Who's in charge here?" No one answers his question. History is full of periods of confusion, war, famine, terror, and conflict. It makes people wonder if anyone is in charge.

Who's in charge? In the eighteenth century, the Enlightenment philosophers declared that human beings have taken control of the world and God had become an amiable and powerless chairman of the board. The human masters of control said they were in charge. In our century they gave us two world wars, the holocaust, the Cambodian killing fields, and the rape of the rain forests in Brazil.

Revelation's answer is that God is in charge of the world and the outcome of history. God gave men and women freedom. They could either make a hell of life on earth, or, with God's grace, make it a place of love, justice, and mercy. Without God, we see what we have done with history. In all other times, these tragedies were occasions for conversion and repentance. They still are, only the voices of Christianity must be raised to issue the call. God is in charge, but he requires our grace-assisted cooperation to move the world toward a positive goal of harmony and reconciliation.

This viewpoint should govern our understanding of the catastrophes John introduces at this point of the narrative. The lamb proceeds to open the seven seals. The event that follows the opening of each seal refers both to an experience in John's time as well as to the end of the world. We can identify the historical connection with biblical times. We have no certain way of saying that a given event in our own day is a sure sign of the Last Judgment.

Every age has the four horsemen of war, ethnic strife, famine, and death. We have had perhaps the worst examples in history of such things. Yet the end of the world did not occur. With the coming of the year 2000 there will be a lot of end-of-the-world talk. The end of Soviet communism and the restoration of Israel are thought by some to be evidence that Jesus is about to return again.

This is pure speculation based on a literalist interpretation of the text and a pre-conceived notion of how the end will happen. We simply do not know. What we do know is that the trials of history and daily life are invitations to faith, conversion, and repentance. We should approach each day we live as though it were our last. We should not engage in futile searches for exact fulfillment of apocalyptic prophecies. Our energy will be better spent improving the world and our spiritual and moral lives.

The White Horse of War (6: 1-2)

The Lamb opens the first seal. It reveals a man on a white horse. The Lamb says, "Come." Bearing the bow of war, the horseman plunges forth, bent on conquest. Some have mistakenly thought the man was Jesus. They confuse this text with Revelation 19:11-12 which tells of a rider on a white horse, whose name is faithful and true. That is clearly Christ. But here the rider is a military figure, carrying the bow of war. The context is a list of woes that will assail the world. The man on the white horse here is not Jesus.

Historically, John may have been thinking of the shocking defeat of the Roman army by the Parthians in A.D. 62. The victorious Parthians, riding their famous white horses, would have held up their bows in triumph. More wars were to come. They would cause suffering for the Christians, along with everyone else. The Romans who were currently causing so much trouble for Christians would themselves face judgment for their cruelty.

The Red Horse of Ethnic Strife (6:3-4)

The second horse is the color of blood. Its rider will take peace away from the earth, this time in the form of ethnic strife and revolutions. John knew well the sad outcome of the abortive revolutions, which the Jews mounted against Rome and the amount of blood that was shed in the streets. He prophesied that this will increase in the near future of his own time and in the last days.

If we look at our own times and think of the blood that was shed or is being shed between Catholics and Protestants in Belfast, in Beirut between Christians and Moslems, in South Africa between whites and blacks, in Cambodia between the Khmer Rouge and their helpless countrymen, in Yugoslavia between Serbs and Croats, in Azerbaijan between Armenians and Azeris – the list seems endless- we might be prompted to think the last days are upon us. But as Jesus reminds us, "Of that day and hour no one knows...but the Father alone" (Mt. 24:36).

The Black Horse of Famine and Economic Crisis (6:5-6)

Now appears the black horse whose rider carries a scale, much like shopkeepers used to weigh food for customers. John hears a voice say, "A ration of wheat costs a day's pay, and three rations of barley costs a day's pay. But do not damage the olive oil or the wine" (verse 6). Where there are food shortages due to famine, crop failure, or inability to deliver the food to the cities, the prices rise. Inflation results. Economic crisis causes all to suffer, the rich who buy wheat and the poor who usually purchase barley.

John prophesies that this will happen when the judgment is made upon those who harass Christians. And this will be one of the major signs that precede the end of the world and the arrival of the Last Judgment. Poverty and hunger will reach an all-time high.

The voice says the oil and the wine will not be damaged. Vines and olive trees have roots that are deeper and so withstand the natural disasters that afflict corn, wheat, and barley crops. Symbolically, the oil and wine refers to the rich whose resources tide them through hard times. Grinding poverty thus lives alongside of immense wealth. Today, rich nations are islands of wealth in a world that has whole continents of poverty. In John's time there were many famines, but Nero and his cronies had plenty of money to buy what was available. The same is true today. Then as now, the gifts of nature are used for the luxury of the few at the expense of the many.

The Pale Horse of Plague and Death (6:7-8)

Lastly, came the pale green horse of plague and death. In the fifteenth century, Albrecht D rer depicted this scene as Father Time – a think bearded judge carrying a three-pronged spear. He is riding at full gallop toward people whose upturned faces look at him with defenseless horror.

In our own time, the Japanese artist Fugita painted the fourth horseman as a skeleton, laughing wildly, riding on the skeleton of a horse across a battlefield strewn with skeletons. A green chlorine cloud of death floats over the scene. Fugita remembers Hiroshima and Nagasaki and uses them to describe this scene from Revelation.

John foresees widespread, violent death caused by plague as another judgment against the sinful who would destroy Christ's kingdom. No person or nation can escape the consequences of sin. "The wages of sin is death" (Rin, 6:23). Sexual promiscuity brings diseases of the flesh. Greed may fill bank accounts, but it empties the soul. Anger that leads to murder also leads to death row. Sloth results in spiritual laziness and dead lives. The sinner incurs the self-destruction that results from sin.

The Fifth Seal: The Tears of the Martyrs (6:9-11)

The Lamb opens the fifth seal and reveals a scene beneath an altar in heaven. We see the souls of the martyrs who were slaughtered because of their faithful witness to Jesus. They wear the white robe of spiritual victory and ask Jesus when he will sit in judgment and "avenge" their blood. This cannot be revenge because that would be contrary to the teaching of Jesus. What they plead for is the restoration of justice in the world and the liberation of Christianity.

They are "beneath the altar." This has two meanings. The heavenly altar images the earthly altars of sacrifice where blood-life was poured out as an offering to God. Christianity no longer has animal sacrifices, but it does have living sacrifices as evidenced in the death of Jesus and the martyrs. We are called to take the cross. We may not be blood martyrs, but we should be "white martyrs," that is, Christians willing to consecrate our lives to sacrificial love for the salvation of the world.

The second meaning refers to the practice of the early Christians who turned the graves of martyrs into altars as can be seen today in the Roman catacombs. This is why relics of saints are embedded in the altars of our parish churches.

The World Falls Apart at the Seams (6:12-17)

The Lamb has heard the cry of the martyrs and answers them in the vision unfolded by the sixth seal. It reveals five pictures which every Jew expected would accompany the day of the Lord and the end of the world.

Earthquake. One prophet after another foresaw the world falling apart when God comes to judge the earth. "On that day there shall be a great shaking… Mountains shall be overturned and cliffs shall tumble, and every wall shall fall to the ground"(Ez. 38:19,20).
Sun and Moon Darkened. The stars…send forth no light; The sun is dark when it rises, and the light of the moon does not shine" (Is. 13:10).

Stars Fall. Nothing makes us more nervous than when the reliability of the earth fails. Biblical people feared that. So do we. Think of our anxiety over the hole in the ozone layer causing cancer-inducing violet rays to attack our skin. The regularity of the heavens is a sign of God's abiding fidelity. Without that we have chaos. When the stars fall, the end is coming.

A Torn Sky. Biblical people imagined the sky as a solid dome. Above it was the "third heaven," where God lived. The dome itself was the second heaven. The sun, moon, stars, and clouds were in the atmosphere of the first heaven. Ripping open the dome – tearing apart the sky – meant that God was coming from the third heaven through the opening to judge the world.

Moveable Mountains. The most solid thing biblical people (including us) could imagine were mountains. Jesus said faith could move a mountain. Before the Last Judgment the last sign of earthly stability would be taken away. Every mountain would be moved from its place.

The following excerpts are from:
Chapter 6, EVENTS PRIOR TO THE FINAL OUTCOME (pp.69-73)
THE NAVARRE BIBLE*, The Book of Revelation* in the Revised Standard Version and **New Vulgate** with a commentary by members of the Faculty of Theology of the University of Navarre. FOUR COURTS PRESS © Text in English from the Revised Standard Version, Catholic Edition [RSVCE] copyrighted 1965 and 1966 by the Division of Christian Education of the National Council of the Churches of Christ in the U.S.A. © SA 1989 First edition 1992

Christ opens the first six seals. Vision of the four horsemen

1 Now I saw when the Lamb opened one of the seven seals, and I heard one of the four living creatures say, as with a voice of thunder, "Come!"

2 And I saw, and behold, a white horse, and its rider had a bow; and a crown was given to him, and he went out conquering and to conquer.

Rev 5:1, 2; 4:6; 5:6, 8 and Zech 1:8-10; 6:1-3

6.1 – 11:14 After describing his vision of heaven, especially the risen Christ empowered to reveal God's hidden plans (chaps. 4-5), the author now begins to disclose that revelation little by little as each of the seven seals is opened(chaps. 6-7). When he comes to the seventh seal, the main one, a new series of visions or revelations begins. These are symbolized by the blowing of the seven trumpets in turn; when the seventh trumpet is sounded (cf. 11:15) the description begins of the last battles fought by Christ and his followers against the powers of evil, the beast and its followers. The sound of the seventh trumpet marks the fulfillment of "the mystery of God". (cf. 10:7).

In its description of the opening of the first six seals, this section covers firstly, the arrival of the day of the wrath of God (cf. 6:17), which is heralded by natural calamities and social upheaval (a foretaste of God's judgment on mankind). This gives the author the opportunity to jump ahead and describe a vision of the saved in heaven. (chap. 7) — putting human history into its proper perspective: all its tragedies and untoward events are a kind of forewarning of the punishment that lies in wait for the evildoer.

The vision then describes another series of catastrophes akin to the plagues of Egypt; preceded by the blowing of trumpets, they herald the coming of God. Like the earlier disasters they are designed to provoke men to a change of heart; because they fail to have any effect, these people will incur God's wrath and will each be judged by him in due course. (cf. 9:20-21; 11:18)

At the end of this section, as a kind of transition to the next, the author stresses the prophetic character of his words: evil seems to have come out winning (as symbolized by the death of the two witnesses: cf. 11:1-13), but this is only apparently so, for Christ, who has already won the victory by his death and resurrection, will be seen to triumph at his second coming. The Lamb will confront the beast and overwhelm it. Until that moment, there is still time for conversion, for opting for or against God. There is no middle course.

3 When he opened the second seal, I heard the second living creature say, "Come!" 4 and out came another horse, Ezek 21:14-16

1-8 The first four seals have various things in common: as they are opened horsemen appear, each of a different colour: and it is always one of the four living creatures which calls up the horsemen. The last three horsemen are easy to identify: the second carries a sword which stands for war; the third a balance, here a symbol of famine, to do with measuring out of rations; and the fourth represents plague, as indicated by the colour of the horse. All three are forms of divine punishment already predicted in the Old Testament: "I will send famine and wild beasts against you, and they will rob you of your children; pestilence and blood shall pass through you; and I will bring the sword upon you. I, the Lord, have spoken" (Ezek 5:17). Jesus used similar language in his eschatological discourse: "And when you hear of wars and tumults, do not be terrified; there will be great earthquakes, and in places famine and pestilence". (Lk 21:9, 11).

The first rider is, however, difficult to interpret: his features suggest that he is some type of power in the service of God. The colour white is symbolic of belonging to the heavenly sphere and of having won victory with God's help (cf 2·7 11, 17, 28; 3;5, 12, etc.), and the bow indicates the connection between this horse and the other three: these latter will be as it were arrows loosed from a distance to implement God's plans. This first rider, who goes forth "conquering and to conquer", refers to Christ's victory in his passion and resurrection, as St. John has already mentioned (cf. 5:5) also announces the final victory of the Word of God which first will come about later (cf. 19:11) The horseman is a kind of key which provides a specifically Christian meaning for all the terrifying events described in the book. Apropos of this figure, Pius XII wrote: "He is Jesus Christ. The inspired evangelist not only saw the devastation brought about by sin, war, hunger and death; he also saw, in the first place, the victory of Christ. It is certainly true that the course the Church takes down through the centuries is a via crucis, a way of the cross, but it is also a victory march. It is the Church of Christ, men and women of Christian faith and love, who are always bringing light, redemption and peace to a mankind without hope. "Jesus Christ, the same yesterday, today and forever"(Heb 13:8)" (Address, 15 November 1946).

4 The sword carried by the rider on the red horse stands for war (cf. Mt 10:34), referring to the wars being waged at the time in the Roman empire, but also to war in general, the scourge of mankind, which at the time of the End will be a signal of the imminent destruction of the world (cf. Mt24:6 and par.).

The Church has had much to say about war in recent times. Thus, the Second Vatican Council says that "insofar as men are sinners, the threat of war hangs over them and will continue until the coming of Christ; but insofar as they can vanquish sin by coming together by charity, violence itself will be vanquished and they will make these words come true: "They shall beat their swords into ploughshares, and their spears into pruning hooks; nation shall not lift up sword again nation, neither shall they learn war anymore" (Is 2:4)"

5 When he opened the third seal, I heard the third living creature say, "Come!" And I saw, and behold, a black horse, and its rider had a balance in his hand ; 6 and I heard what seemed to be a voice in the midst of the four living creatures saying, " A quart of wheat for a denarius, and three quarts of barley for a denarius; but do not harm oil and wine!"   (Ezk 4:16f and 1 Kings 6:25f)

5-6 A sudden (perhaps tenfold) rise in the price of wheat and barley, part of the staple diet at the time, signals a period of famine. If we bear in mind that a "quart" (Greek: choinix) was about one kilo or 30 ounces and a denariusa day's wages for a labourer (cf.Mt 20:13), these are clearly very high prices. Famine and hunger are clearly a consequence of sin and therefore can be interpreted as a "punishment". The Church reminds us all that we have a strict duty to alleviate the needs of others, for this is a way of combating evil. "The Council asks individuals and governments to remember the saying of the Fathers:"

Feed the man dying of hunger, because if you do not feed him you are killing him" (Gratian, Decretum, 21, 86) and it urges them according to their ability to share and dispose of their goods to help others, above all by giving them aid which will enable them to help and develop themselves." (Gaudium et spes, 69).

7 When he opened the fourth seal, I heard the voice of the fourth living creature say, "Come!" 8 And I saw, and behold a pale horse and its rider's name was Death, and Hades followed him and they were given power over a fourth of the earth, to kill with sword and with famine and with pestilence and by wild beasts of the earth. Hos 13:14, Ezk 5:12;14:12; Jer 14:12

When he opened the fifth seal, I saw under the altar the souls of those who had been slain for the word of God and for the witness they had borne; 10 they cried out with a loud voice, O Sovereign Lord, holy and true, how long before thou wilt judge and avenge our blood on those who dwell upon the earth?" 11 Then they were each given a white robe and told to rest a little longer, until the number of their fellow servants and their brethren should be complete, who were to be killed as they themselves had been.

All this is meant to show that in the midst of all the terrible chastisement God has pity on mankind: most (three quarters, that is) will manage to survive the test.

9-11 Here St. John sees all who gave their lives for God. The vision takes in the Old Testament martyrs from Abel down to Zechariah (cf. Mt 23: 35-37; Heb 11:35-40), and Christian martyrs of all eras; St John see them under the altar of holocausts where victims were sacrificed in honour of God and their blood collected beneath. Here we see a heavenly copy of that altar, meaning that the martyrs are very close to God and that their death has been a most respectable offering to him (cf. Phil 2:17; 2 Tim 4:6).

The presence of the martyrs in heaven shows that when man dies his soul receives its reward or punishment immediately. God's judgment of each soul begins to take effect the moment he dies, although it is not until the resurrection of the dead that it will have its full effect, on body as well as soul.

The martrys' song is a clamour for justice: our Lord refers to it in the Gospel (cf. Lk 18:7) and it echoes the aboriginal lament raised at Abel's death (cf. Gen 4:10). What the martyrs say seems to be at odds with Christ's prayer on the cross (cf. Lk 23:24) and Stephen's on the eve of his martyrdom (cf. Act 7:60), but there is really no contradiction. "This prayer of the martyrs", St Thomas says, "is nothing other than their desire to obtain resurrection of the body and to share in the inheritance of those who will be saved, and their recognition of God's justice in punishing evildoers" (Summa theologiae, III, q. 72, a. 3, ad. 1).

It is, thus, a prayer for the establishment of the Kingdom of God and his justice, which causes his divine holiness and fidelity to shine forth.

12 When he opened the sixth seal, I looked, and behold, there was a great earthquake; and the sun became black as sackcloth, the full moon became like blood, 13 and the stars of the sky fell to the earth as the fig tree sheds its winter fruit when shaken by a gale, 14 the sky vanished like a scroll that is rolled up, and every mountain and island was removed from its place.

15 Then the kings of the earth and great men and the generals and the rich and the strong, and every one, slave and free, hid in the caves among the rocks of the mountains, 16 calling to the mountains and rocks, "Fall on us and hide us from the face of him who is seated on the throne, and from the wrath of the Lamb; 17 for the great day of their wrath has come, and who can stand before it?".

12-17 This passage predicts the events which will occur just before the second coming of our Lord Jesus Christ. It does not refer to the very End, but to the fact that it is imminent. The terrifying symbols used to indicate these events derive from literary style and language used in the Old Testament (cf., e.g., Amos 8:9; Is 13:98f; 34:4; 50:3 Job 3:4) This was the prophets' way of warning the people---and of consoling them by telling them that Christ's definitive victory would soon come. Jesus speaks in the same way to the grieving women of Jerusalem whom he meets on his way to Calvary (cf. Lk 23:30)

In v. 15 there is a reference to seven social groups embracing all mankind, ranging from the highest to the lowest. Nothing escapes God's judgment and there is no appeal against it. The Dies Irae has come, the day of the Lamb's wrath. The Lamb symbolizes the innocence and immolation of the Messiah; but it also stands for messianic royalty, symbolized here by his fury.

The great multitude of the saved

1 After this I saw four angels standing at the four corners of the earth, holding back the four winds of the earth, that no wind might blow on earth or sea or against any tree.

2 Then I saw another angel ascend from the rising of the sun, with the seal of the living God, and he called with a loud voice to the four angels who had been given power to harm earth and sea, 3 saying "Do not harm the earth or the sea or the trees, till we have sealed the servants of our God upon their foreheads." 4 And I heard the number of the sealed, out of every tribe of the sons of Israel, 5 twelve thousand of the tribe of Judah, twelve thousand of the tribe of Reuben, twelve thousand of the tribe of Gad, 6 twelve thousand of the tribe of Asher, twelve thousand of the tribe of Naphtali, twelve thousand of the tribe of Manasseh, 7 twelve thousand of the tribe of Simeon, twelve thousand of the tribe of Levi, twelve thousand of the tribe of Issachar, 8 twelve thousand of the tribe of Zebulun, twelve thousand of the tribe of Joseph, twelve thousand sealed out of the tribe of Benjamin.

1-17 This chapter consists of two visions designed to illustrate God's protection of Christians and the happy circumstances of the martyrs. The victory of the Church is depicted—of the entire Church, made up of people from the four points of the compass (vv. 9-12). What is not so clear, however, is who the one hundred and forty four thousand are, drawn from the twelve tribes of Israel, whom an angel has marked with the seal of the living God (vv. 1-8). Some commentators interpret them as all being Christians of Jewish background (Judaeo-Christians). Others say that they are those who make up the new Israel which St Paul speaks about in Galatians 6:17: that is, all the baptized viewed first as still engaged in their battle (vv. 1-8) and then after they have won victory (vv. 9-17). The most plausible interpretation is that the one hundred and forty four thousand stand for the Jews converted to Christianity (as distinct from those not converted)—the 'remnant of Israel' (cf. Is 4:2-4: Ezek 9; etc). St Paul says that they prove the irrevocable nature of God's election (cf. Rom 11:1-5) and are the first-fruits of the restoration which will come about at the End (cf. Rom 11:25-32).

The hundred and forty-four thousand are included in the second vision; they would be part of the great multitude "from all tribes and people and tongues". Thus, the vision in vv. 9-17 takes in the entire Church without any distinctions, whereas the vision in vv. 1-8 can refer only to a part of the Church—those Jews who, by becoming Christians, made up the original nucleus of the Church. The Church admits these on the same basis as all those who become Christians later without having had to pass through any stage of Jewish observance.

1-8 In Jewish tradition angels were divided into two groups—angels of the Presence and sanctification, and those charged with controlling the forces of nature. Both kinds appear in this passage.

According to the custom of the time, when something bore the mark of a seal or brand that meant that it belonged to the seal's owner. This passage is saying that the one hundred and forty four thousand belong to God and therefore will be protected by him as his property. This fulfils what Ezekiel prophesied about the inhabitants of Jerusalem (cf. Ezek 9:1-7): some would be sealed on the forehead with a tau (the last letter of the Hebrew alphabet) and would therefore escape the punishment to be inflicted on all the rest: this shows the special way God makes provision for those who are his not only because he created them but also by a new title.

The Fathers of the Church saw this mark as symbolizing the character Baptism impresses on the souls of the faithful to show that they are destined for eternal life. Thus, the persons preserved from harm are the Jews who were converts to Christianity: their Baptism marked them out from those Jews who rejected Christ and were not baptized.

The list of tribes is somewhat different from the usual list which keeps the order of Genesis 29. The name of Judah is put first because the Messiah came from that tribe, as St John recently mentioned (cf. 5:5); and there is no mention of the tribe of Dan, presumably because it fell into idolatry (cf. Judg 17-18) and eventually disappeared. To make up the tally of twelve the tribe of Joseph is mentioned twice— or that of Joseph and as that of Manasseh, his first-born.

The number of those sealed (12 x 12 x 1000) symbolizes completeness, totality— in this instance, a huge multitude, depicted as the new Israel. Included in this number are the descendants of Jacob who receive Baptism, irrespective of when they do. Obviously this number is not meant to be taken literally, as if only one hundred and forty-four thousand people will attain salvation. In this scene all those of Gentile background who become Christians over the course of history are explicitly not included. They will appear in the vision which follows.

9 After this I looked, and behold, a great multitude which no man could number, from every nation, from all tribes and peoples and tongues, standing before the throne and before the Lamb, clothed in white robes, with palm branches in their hands, 10 and crying out with a loud voice, "Salvation belongs to our God who sits upon the throne, and to the Lamb!"

11 And all the angels stood round the throne and round the elders and the four living creatures, and they fell on their faces before the throne and worshipped God, 12 saying, "Amen! Blessing and glory and wisdom and thanksgiving and honour and power and might be to our God forever and ever! Amen."

13 Then one of the elders addressed me, say, "Who are these, clothed in white robes, and whence have they come?" 14 I said to him, "Sir, you know." And he said to me, "These are they who have come out of the great tribulation; they have washed their robes and made them white in the blood of the Lamb.

15 Therefore are they before the throne of God, and serve him day and night within his temple; and he who sits upon the throne will shelter them with his presence.

16 They shall hunger no more, neither thirst anymore; the sun shall not strike them, not any scorching heat.

17 For the Lamb in the midst of the throne will be their shepherd, and he will guide them to springs of living water; and God will wipe away every tear from their eyes."

9-17 Pope John Paul II has commented on this passage as follows: "The people dressed in white robes whom John sees with his prophetic eye are the redeemed, and they from a great multitude', which no one could count and which is made up of people of the most varied backgrounds. They blood of the Lamb, who has been offered in sacrifice for all, has exercised its universal and most effective redemptive power in every corner of the earth, extending grace and salvation to that 'great multitude'. After undergoing the trials and being purified in the blood of Christ, they—the redeemed—are now safe in the Kingdom of God, whom they praise and bless for ever and ever" (Homily, 1 November 1981). This great crowd includes all the saved and not just the martyrs, for it says that they washed their robes in the blood of the Lamb, not in their own blood.

Everyone has to become associated with Christ's passion through suffering, as St Augustine explains, not without a certain humour: "Many are martyrs in their beds. The Christian is lying on his couch, tormented by pain. He prays and his prayers are not heard, or perhaps they are heard but he is being put to the test…so that he may be received as a son. He becomes a martyr through illness and is crowned by him who hung upon the Cross" (Sermon 286, 8).

"It is consoling and encouraging to know that those who attain heaven constitute a huge multitude. The passages of Matthew 7:14 and Luke 13:24 which seem to imply that very few will be saved should be interpreted in the light of this vision, which shows that the infinite value of Christ's blood makes God's will be done: "(God) desires all men to be saved and to come to the knowledge of the truth" (1 Tim 2:4)

In vv 14-17 we see the blessed in two different situations—first, before the resurrection of the body (v. 14) and, then, after it, when body and soul have been reunited (vv. 15-17). In this second situation the nature of risen bodies is highlighted: they cannot suffer pain or inconvenience of any kind: they are out of harm's reach; they have the gift of "impassibility" (cf. St Pius V Catechism 1, 12, 13).

This consoling scene is included in the vision to encourage believers to imitate those Christians who were like us and now find themselves in heaven because they have come through victorious. The Church invites us to pray along similar lines: "Father, you sanctified the Church of Rome with the blood of its first martyrs. May we find strength from their courage and rejoice in their triumph" (Roman Missal, Feast of the First Martyrs of the Church of Rome, opening prayer).

The opening of the seventh seal

8:1 When the Lamb opened the seventh seal, there was silence in heaven for about half an hour.

2 Then I saw the seven angels who stand before God, and seven trumpets were given to them.

3 And another angel came and stood at the altar with a golden censer; and he was given much incense to mingle with the prayers of all the saints upon the golden altar before the throne; 4and the smoke of the incense rose with

the prayers of the saints from the hand of the angel before God. 5 Then the angel took the censer and filled it with fire from the altar and threw it on the earth; and there were peals of thunder, loud noises, flashes of lightning, and an earthquake.

6 Now the seven angels who had the seven trumpets made ready to blow them. The first six trumpet calls. The three woes

7 The first angel blew his trumpet, and there followed hail and fire, mixed with blood, which fell on the earth; and a third of the earth burnt up, and a third of the trees were burnt up, and all green grass was burnt up.

1-2. The silence is a signal that the End has come: it expresses the Lord's patient waiting—as if he were putting off the day of judgment, to the chagrin of the faithful. However, "the Lord is not slow about his promise as some count slowness, but is forebearing toward you, not wishing that any should perish, but that all should reach repentance" (2 Pet 3:9).

The opening of the seventh seal leads to another "seven", the seven trumpets; and the last of these leads to the seven bowls (cf. Rev 11:15). But first we are told what happens when the first six trumpets are blown (chap. 8-9) and God's judgments are visited on the earth. There is a certain parallel here with the plagues of Egypt (cf. Ex 7:14 – 12:34). Before the seventh trumpet is sounded, there is a sort of interlude (cf. 10:1 – 11:14).

Trumpets were used by the Israelites not only in battle (cf. Josh 6:5) but also in the temple liturgy, where they proclaimed the presence of Yahweh (cf. Ps 47:6). In accounts of our Lord's second coming we find references to trumpets being sounded to signal that divine intervention is imminent (cf., e.g. Mt 24:31; 1 Cor 15:52, 1 Thess 4:15).

3-5 The prayers of the saints, previously identified by bowls of incense (cf. 5:8), are now mingled with the aromatic incense rising from the golden censer. All this is a reference to the fact that the saints in heaven intercede with God on our behalf. The Second Vatican Council reminds us that "the Church has always believed that the apostles and Christ's martyrs, who gave the supreme witness of faith and charity by the shedding of their blood, are closely united with us in Christ; she has always venerated them, together with the Blessed Virgin Mary and the holy angels, with a special love, and has asked piously for the help of their intercession" (Lumen gentium, 50). The Council of Trent recommends that the faithful be taught how profitable it is to have recourse to the intercession of the saints: "it is a good and useful thing to invoke the saints humbly and to have recourse to their prayers" (De sacris imaginibus).

The usefulness of intercessory prayer is something we learn about first in the Old Testament. For example, we are told how Moses, with his hands raised to heaven, pleaded successfully for Israelite victory over the Amalekites (cf. Ex

17:8f). Also, the references here to the altar of incense recall elements of Jewish worship (cf. Ex 29:13, Lev 21:6, Ps 141:2: etc), which was a prefiguration of the worship "in spirit and truth" (Jn 4:23) announced by Jesus.

In response to the prayers of the saints, the Lord once again manifests his presence in the way he did at Sinai (cf. not on 4:5). The angel's action is reminiscent of Ezekiel 10:2, where the angel fills his hands with burning coals and scatters them over Jerusalem. This rain of fire now signals the start of God's fury on the world and on mankind, which is described here in stages marked by trumpet blasts.

6-12 The blowing of the first four trumpets is separated from that of the following ones by a vision (v. 13); the same pattern applied to the seven seals. The punishments the trumpet calls herald are reminiscent of the plagues of Egypt. No necessary historical sequence of events is being described here; the order is more logical than historical. Each successive divine intervention is simply a further manifestation of God's power and justice. The devastation which the trumpets introduce is greater than that produced by the opening of the first four seals: a third of the earth is affected, not just a quarter (cf. 6:8). Divine mercy, however, still controls the range of the punishment and prevents total annihilation.

8 The second angel blew his trumpet, and something like a great mountain, burning with fire, was thrown into the sea; 9 and a third of the sea became blood, a third of the living creatures in the sea died, and a third of the ships were destroyed.

10 The third angel blew his trumpet, and a great star fell from heaven, blazing like a torch, and it fell on a third of the rivers and on the fountains of water.

11 The name of the star is Wormwood. A third of the waters became wormwood, and many men died of the water, because it was made bitter.

12 The fourth angel blew his trumpet, and a third of the sun was struck, and a third of the moon, and a third of the stars, so that a third of their light was darkened; a third of the day was kept from shining, and likewise a third of the night.

13 Then I looked, and I heard an eagle crying with a loud voice, as it flew in midheaven, "Woe, woe, woe to those who dwell on the earth, at the blasts of the other trumpets which the three angels are about to blow!"

Following the logical order which classifies the cosmos into land, sea and sky, the blowing of the first trumpet affects the vegetation (v. 7); the description is parallel to the account of the seventh plague in Exodus 9:13-35.

The blowing of the two next trumpets affects seas and rivers (vv. 10-11). Many perish as a result of the pollution of the waters. Both these calamities are connected with the first plague of Egype [sic] (cf. Ex 7:19-21).

After this contamination of land and sea, the heavens are affected by the fourth trumpet. The sun and the heavenly bodies are darkened, so that their power is reduced by a third: these effects are reminiscent to some degree of Exodus 10:21-29.

13 This passage is a short break before the last three trumpet calls. The lament of the eagle, which may stand for an angel, can be heard all over the world. Its "woe, woe, woe" expresses horror and compassion at the events which follow. This cannot fail to impress the reader, it creates an atmosphere of foreboding. "Those who dwell on earth": a reference to idolaters (cf. Rev 3:10, who are persecuting Christians. It does not refer to the faithful but only to those who have let themselves be led astray by Christ's enemies (cf. Rev 6:10, 11:10; 13:8, 12,14; 17:2-8).

9:1 – 11:19. The next two trumpets will impact directly on mankind, producing more horrific effects, in a kind of crescendo. These trumpets follow one after the other (9:1-21), whereas there is a delay before the blowing of the seventh (11:15-19), during which a number of visions occur (10:1 – 11:14) which anticipate later events narrated in chapters 12-22.

1-2 The commonest interpretation of the star fallen from heaven to earth is that it stands for one of the fallen angels, most likely Satan himself, of whom Christ said, "I saw Satan fall like lightning from heaven" (Lk 10-18) and whom the present text later describes as being thrown down to the earth (cf. note on 12:13). Behind this lies the notion that the demons are incarcerated in the bowels of the earth. The writer is being thrown down to the earth the writer is trying to convey the idea that, when the fifth trumpet is blown, God is going to let demoniacal forces loose to wreak havoc on those of mankind who refuse to recognize God (cf. v. 4). They will be free to operate only for a limited period and to a limited degree and will have to obey "the angel of the bottomless pit" (v. 11), who would be the same angel as received the key of the shafts of the abyss (v. 9), the prince of the demons. Very near the end of the Apocalypse the writer sees the other side of the coin, as it were—Satan and his followers being shut up once more in the pit, after Christ's victory (cf. 20:1-3).

9:1 And the fifth angel blew his trumpet, and I saw a star fallen from heaven to earth, and he was given the key of the shaft of the bottomless pit; 2 he opened the shaft of the bottomless pit, and from the shaft rose smoke like the smoke of a great furnace, and the sun and the air were darkened with the smoke from the shaft.

3 Then from the smoke came locusts on the earth, and they were given power like the power of scorpions of the earth; 4 they were told not to harm the grass of the earth or any green growth or any tree, but only those of mankind who

have not the seal of God upon their foreheads; 5 they were allowed to torture them for five months, but not to kill them, and their torture was like the torture of a scorpion, when it stings a man. 6 And in those days men will seek death and will not find it; they will long to die, and death will fly from them.

7 In appearance the locusts were like horses arrayed for battle; on their heads were what looked like crowns of gold; their faces were like human faces, 8 their hair like women's hair, and their teeth like lions' teeth; 9 they had scales like iron breastplates, and the noise of their wings was like the noise of many chariots with horses rushing into battle.

10 They have tails like scorpions, and stings, and their power or hurting men for five months lies in their tails.

11 They have as king over them the angel of the bottomless pit; his name in Hebrew is Abaddon, and in Greek he is called Apollyon.

12 The first woe has passed; behold, two woes are still to come.

13 Then the sixth angel blew his trumpet, and I heard a voice from the four horns of the golden altar before God, 14 saying to the sixth angel who had the trumpet, "Release the four angels who are bound at the great river Euphrates."

15 So the four angels were released, who had been held ready for the hour, the day, the month, and the year, to kill a third of mankind.

16 The number of the troops of cavalry was twice ten thousand times ten thousand; I heard their number.

17 And this was how I saw the horses in my vision: the riders wore breastplates the colour of fire and of sapphire and of sulphur, and the heads of the horses were like lions' heads, and fire and smoke and sulphur issued from their mouths.

18 By these three plagues a third of mankind was killed, by the fire and smoke and sulphur issuing from their mouths.

19 For the power of the horses is in their mouths and in their tails; their tails are like serpents, with heads, and by means of them they wound.

20 The rest of mankind, who were not killed by these plagues, did not repent of the works of their hands nor give up worshipping demons and idols of gold and silver and bronze and stone and wood, which cannot either see or hear or walk; 21 nor did they repent of their murders or their sorceries or their immorality or their thefts.

3-6 In order to describe the demons and the havoc they create, St John evokes the eighth plague of Egypt, the plague of locusts (cf. Ex 10:14 ff), making it clear, however, that this plague is much more horrific and on another level altogether. It will do such grievous harm to men that they will wish they were dead but they will have to endure it for a fixed amount of time: the "five months", the life-time of the locust, conveys the idea that these afflictions will last for a limited time.

7-12 The description of the locusts is designed to show how terrifying demons are; cf. the prophet Joel's description of the invading army (Joel 1:2-2:17). The crowns of gold identify them as conquerors; their faces, as creatures with intelligence; their hairiness and loins' teeth symbolize ferocity; their iron breastplates show them to be fully armed warriors; and the noise they create and their scorpion tails show their extreme cruelty. They obey a leader, Satan, whose name (Abaddon, Apollyon) denotes destruction and extermination. His name contrasts with that of Jesus, which means "Yahweh saves".

13-19 As before, God permits the angels of evil to have their way; he uses them to inflict just punishment and offer the rest of mankind a chance to repent of their sins (vv. 20-21). The golden altar standing before the throne of God is shaped like the altar of the temple of Jerusalem (cf. Ex 37:26; Amos 3:14), with its four prominent corners and four horns; from the midst of the horns comes the voice which sets these punishments in motion.

The inspired writer now describes a new and dreadful vision. The vast size of the cavalry shows the scale of the evil in the world. The river Euphrates (in a sense the frontier of the world of the Bible) was the direction from which invasions of Israel usually came (cf. Is 7:20; Jer 46:10; etc). At the time of writing it was the region from which the Parthians mounted their threat to the Roman empire.

Some of the details of the vision are reminiscent of other descriptions of ruin and desolation (cf. Gen 19:24-28) and of monstrous animals (cf. Job 41:11). Fire, smoke and sulphur all indicate that this army of monsters originates in hell.

20-21 In the last analysis, as shown here, all the punishments described in the Book of Revelation are designed to move people to repentance. That was also the thrust of the letters to the seven churches (cf. Rev 2:5, 16, 21; 3:3; etc). But the author shows that people persist in turning away from God to worship idols, which are really only scarecrows compared with Yahweh, the living God (cf. e.g., Ps 113; Jer 10:3-5).

In the last analysis idolatry is the root of all other sins: by turning his back on God man comes under the control of the forces of evil (forces within him as well as outside him) which push him to commit all kinds of sins and perversions. St Paul deals with the same idea in his Letter to the Romans where he says that by cutting themselves off from God men are given over to their own passions and commit most abominable sins (cf. Rom 1:18-32).

The author is given the little scroll to eat

1 Then I saw another mighty angel coming down from heaven, wrapped in a cloud, with a rainbow over his head, and his face was like the sun, and his legs like pillars of fire. 2 He had a little scroll open in his hand. And he set his right foot on the sea, and his left foot on the land, 3 and called out with a loud voice, like a lion roaring; when he called out, the seven thunders sounded.

4 And when the seven thunders had sounded, I was about to write, but I heard a voice from heaven saying, "Seal up what the seven thunders have said, and do not write it down."

5 And the angel whom I saw standing on the sea and land lifted up his right hand to heaven, 6 and swore by him who lives for ever and ever, who created heaven and what is in it, the earth and what is in it, and the sea and what is in it, that there should be no more delay, 7 but that in the days of the trumpet call to be sounded by the seventh angel, the mystery of God, as he announced to his servants the prophets, should be fulfilled.

8 Then the voice which I had heard from heaven spoke to me again, saying, "Go, take the scroll which is open in the hand of the angel who is standing on the sea and on the land." 9So I went to the angel and told him to give me the little scroll; and he said to me, "Take it and eat; it will be bitter to your stomach, but sweet as honey in your mouth." 10And I took the little scroll from the hand of the angel and ate it; it was sweet as honey in my mouth, but when I had eaten it my stomach was made bitter. 11And I was told "You must again prophesy about many peoples and nations and tongues and kings."

God inflicts punishment in order to bring about the conversion of sinners. Sometimes, however, the end result is that they become more obdurate. That was the case with Pharaoh; when the plagues struck Egypt, far from repenting, he persecuted the Israelites more bitterly than ever, Divine punishment, then, has a medicinal and exemplary purpose and is good for everyone without exception. In the Gospel Jesus tells us that the Galileans whom Pilate put to death, and the people who perished when the tower collapsed on them in Siloam, were not more blameworthy than other people, and therefore we too will perish unless we repent (cf. Lk 13:1-5).

1 After the events following the sixth trumpet call (cf. 9:13-21) and before the seventh (cf. 11:15), we are shown a new vision (as an aside, as it were). The seer is once again back on earth, as he was when the letters were being dispatched (cf. 10:4; 1:4 – 3:22), whereas he sees the "trumpet" visions from the vantage point of heaven (chaps. 4-9 and 12). This shows that we are dealing here with an aside which is designed to prepare the reader for the seventh and final trumpet blast.

In this "out of sequence" vision St John reminds us of his prophetic role by bringing in the symbolic action of eating a little scroll (cf. 10:8-11) and recalling the testimony of the ancient prophets, who are represented by the two witnesses (cf. 11:1 10).

Although the angel is not named, he may be Gabriel: he is described as "mighty" (geber, in Hebrew), and Gabriel (gabri'el, in Hebrew) means "strength of God" or "man of God" (cf. Dan 8:15) or "God shows his strength". Be that as it may, Gabriel is the name given to the angel charged with explaining the messianic prophecies to Daniel and with communicating divine messages to Zechariah (cf. Lk 1:19) and to the Blessed Virgin (cf. Lk 1:26). He performed a function parallel to that of the angel who appears in 8:3-5 and who is usually identified as St Michael. The way he is described emphasizes his heavenly character and his strength.

2 The open scroll carried by the angel is different from the sealed scroll in the vision recounted in Revelation 5:2. It is more like the scroll described by the prophet Ezekiel (cf. Ezek 2:9 – 3:1) which was also meant to be eaten by the seer. The fact that it is open indicates that its content is not secret. The eating of the scroll symbolizes that what the prophet has to say after he eats it is really the work of God. It also indicates that God speaks through the medium of a written text. So, this imagery helps to strengthen people's faith in the divine inspiration of sacred writing, that is, the Bible, and to recognize them for what they are—holy books because they are the very work of God which reaches the Church in written form via inspired authors: by reading these books publicly the Church is in fact proclaiming their divine inspiration.

We are not told what this little scroll contains; so, the only reason the writer brings in this symbol is to make it clear that he is a prophet. He wants people to be in no doubt about the fact that his prophecies apply to all creation—both heaven and earth (v.6).

3-7 Like the voice of God in the Old Testament, the angel's voice is here compared to the roar of a lion (cf. Hos 11:10, Amos 1:2. 3:8) and to thunder (cf. Is 29:6) which strikes fear into men.

According to the text each peal of thunder carries a message of its own; and the fact of there being seven means that they carry everything God wishes to reveal. However, the content of this revelation is not to be communicated further and will only be made known at the end of time. The sealing of the scroll shows that this revelation is to be kept secret and that there is no point in anyone trying to discover it. It is part of the mystery which God chooses to keep hidden—in the same way as we do not known when our Lord's second coming and the end of the world will be (cf. Mt 24:36).

The angel's gesture and solemn oath assured the seer that the definitive establishment of the Kingdom of God will come about when there will be "no more delay", no more time, for the world in its present form. However, as to the timing, all that is said is that it will happen when the mystery of God (his plan of salvation) has reached its final climax, when the harvest-time has come (cf. Mt 13:24-30) and good and evil—wheat and weeds—will be clear for all to see (cf. 2 Thess 2:6ff).

In the Apocalypse, the end of time is signaled by the blowing of the seventh trumpet (described later:cf. 11:15) which will mark fulfillment to "three woes" which is a motive of hope for the Church and a call to conversion for all mankind: "But do not ignore this one fact, beloved, that with the Lord one day is as a thousand years, and a thousand years as one day. The Lord is not slow about his promise as some count slowness, but is forbearing toward you, not wishing that any should perish, but that all should reach repentance" (2 Pet 3:8-9)

8-11 Cf. note on 10:2. The book described by Ezekiel 2:8 -3:3 was sweet as honey when eaten; but when Ezekiel began to prophesy, his heart was filled with bitterness (cf. Ezek 3:14). The same symbolism of the two kinds of taste is used here—no doubt to indicate that the prophecy contains grace and blessing, and also judgment and condemnation. The sweetness can also be interpreted as reflecting the triumph of the Church, and the bitterness its afflictions.

"You must again prophesy about many peoples and nations and tongues and kings."

The death and resurrection of the two witnesses

1 Then I was given a measuring rod like a staff, and I was told: "Rise and measure the temple of God and the altar and those who worship there, 2 but do not measure the court outside the temple; leave that out, for it is given over to the nations, and they will trample over the holy city for forty-two months. 3 And I will grant my two witnesses power to prophesy for one thousand two hundred and sixty days, clothed in sackcloth.:

Although nothing is said about what is written on the scroll John is given to eat, it is reasonable to suppose that it has to do with the passage about the two witnesses which now follows, before the blowing of the seventh trumpet; this would make it a prophetic oracle, brought in here as a preview of the final eschatological battles, to show that evil apparently triumphs on earth.

The death and resurrection of the two witnesses

1 Then I was given a measuring rod like a staff, and I was told: "Rise and measure the temple of God and the altar and those who worship there, 2 but do not measure the court outside the temple; leave that out, for it is given over to the nations, and they will trample over the holy city for forty-two months.

3 And I will grant my two witnesses power to prophesy for one thousand two hundred and sixty days, clothed in sackcloth."

4 These are the two olive trees and the two lampstands which stand before the Lord of the earth. 5 And if anyone would harm them, fire pours from their mouth and consumes their foes; if anyone would harm them, thus he is doomed to be killed.

6 They have power to shut the sky, that no rain may fall during the days of their prophesying, and they have power over the waters to turn them into blood, and to smite the earth with every plague, as often as they desire.

7 And when they have finished their testimony, the beast that ascends from the bottomless pit will make war upon them and conquer them and kill them, 8 and their dead bodies will lie in the street of the great city which is allegorically called Sodom and Egypt, where their Lord was crucified.

9 For three days and a half men from the peoples and tribes and tongues and nations gaze at their dead bodies and refuse to let them be placed in a tomb, 10 and those who dwell on earth will rejoice over them and make merry and exchange presents, because these two prophets had been a torment to those who dwell on the earth. 11 But after the three and a half days a breath of life from God entered them, and they stood up on their feet, and great fear fell on those who saw them.

12 Then they heard a loud voice from heaven saying to them, "Come up hither!" And in the sight of their foes they went up to heaven in a cloud.

13 And at that hour there was a great earthquake, and a tenth of the city fell; seven thousand people were killed in the earthquake, and the rest were terrified and gave glory to the God of heaven. 14 The second woe has passed; behold, the third woe is soon to come.

The sounding of the seventh trumpet

15 Then the seventh angel blew his trumpet, and there were loud voices in heaven, saying, "The kingdom of the world has become the kingdom of our Lord and of his Christ, and he shall reign forever and ever." 16 And the twenty-four elders who sit on their thrones before God fell on their faces and worshipped God, 17 saying,"We give thanks to thee, Lord God Almighty, who art and who wast, that thou hast taken thy great power and begun to reign.

18 The nations raged, but thy wrath came, and the time for the dead to be judged, for rewarding thy servants, the prophets and saints, and those who fear thy name, both small and great, and for destroying the destroyers of the earth."

19 Then God's temple in heaven was opened, and the ark of his covenant was seen within his temple; and there were flashes of lightning, loud noises, peals of thunder, an earthquake, and heavy hail.

1-13 The prophecy connected with what is on the scroll (11:1-13) acts as a preamble to the events that follow the blowing of the seventh and last trumpet (11;15ff). It has to do with the tribulation suffered by the Church (the Church is symbolized by the temple of Jerusalem and its altar). The ultimate cause of this suffering is the forces of evil, that is, the beast (antichrist) which makes its appearance in the Holy City (cf 11:17). In the course of a limited period, that is, the history of mankind, there are moments when the forces of evil prevail and many people transgress God's law. The witnesses of the true God come forward to preach penance (11:3-6) and are martyred to the great delight of their adversaries (cf. 11:7-10). But God intervenes on behalf of these martyrs, taking them up into heaven and decimating their foes; the terrified survivors submit to God (cf. 11:11-13).

This prophetic teaching echoes what we are told in the Second Letter to the Thessalonians: "Let no one deceive you in any way; for that day will not come unless the rebellion comes first, and the man of lawlessness is revealed, the son of perdition, who opposes and exalts himself against every so-called god or object of worship, so that he takes his seat in the temple of God, proclaiming himself to be God" (2 Thess 2:3-4). Using Old Testament imagery and language the author of Revelation is pointing out, as Jesus did (cf. Mk 13:14-32), that the destruction of Jerusalem and the castrophies which accompany it are a sign and symbol of the end of the world and a warning to everyone (particularly the Jewish people) who are called as the Jews are, to share in the salvation brought by Christ (cf. Rom 11:25-26).

1-2 The image of the measuring rod is taken from the prophet Ezekiel but it is used in a different way: it shows God is going to preserve part of the Holy City from the destructive power of the Gentiles. This part stands for the Church, the community of those who worship god in spirit and in truth (cf. Jn 4:23).

Jerusalem was trampled underfoot by the Gentiles in the time of Antiochus Epiphanes, who profaned the temple and installed in it a statue of Zeus Olympus (cf. 1 Mac 1:54;); worse destruction still was done by the Romans, who destroyed both temple and city, leaving not a stone upon a stone (Mt 24:21; Mk 13:14-23; Lk 21:20-24). Taking his cue from these events, St John prophesies that the Church will never suffer the same fate, for God protects it from the power of its enemies (cf. Mt 16:16-18). Christians may suffer persecution in one way or another, but physical or moral violence cannot overpower the Church, because God protects it. "The Church, 'like a stranger in a foreign land, presses forward amid the persecutions of the world and the consolations of God' (St Augustine, The City of God, 18,51), announcing the cross and death of the Lord until he comes (cf. 1 Cor 11:26). But by the power of the risen Lord it is given strength to overcome, in patience and in love, its sorrows and its difficulties, both those that are from within and those that are from without, so that it may reveal in the world, faithfully, however darkly, the mystery of its Lord until, in the consummation, it shall be manifested in full light" (Vatican II, *Lumen gentium*, 8).

The forty-two months established as the period during which the Gentiles will trample on the Holy City stand for the length of the persecution. This is a symbolic number equivalent to three and a half years or "a time, times and half a time" (12:13), that is, "a half week of years" – half seven-which stands for an incomplete, that is limited, period of time. Perfect, complete time is symbolized by the figure seven (cf. Gen 1:2 – 2:3) or by seventy (cf. Dan 9:24). The prophet Daniel uses the same symbolism to indicate the duration of persecution (cf. Dan 7:25; 12:7); the author of the Apocalypse puts it to the same purpose here and in the next verse, where the same period is expressed in terms of days (one thousand two hundred and sixty): the period stands for the duration of the Church's sufferings in the course of history (cf. Rev 12:6, 14; 13:5): this period is of limited duration, merely a prelude to the definitive victory of Christ and his Church.

3-6 The period of tribulation coincides with the length of time the two witnesses prophesy. They call people to penance (symbolized by their use of sackcloth). God protects them in a very special way; and yet he does not spare them death or suffering; in the end, however, they will be glorified in heaven. In the Apocalypse the identity of the two witnesses is not given; they are referred to as "olive trees" –the same language as used of Zerubbabel, a prince of the line of David, and Joshua, the high priest (cf. Zech 3:3-14). But they are assigned features of Elijah, who brought about a drought (cf. 1 Kings 17:1-13; 18:10, and Moses, who turned the Nile to blood (cf. Ex 7:14-16). The enemies of Elijah and Moses were also devoured by fire from heaven (cf. 2 Kings 17:1-10; Num 16:35). However, because the two witnesses testify to Jesus Christ and die martyrs, tradition identifies them with St Peter and St Paul, who suffered martyrdom in Rome, the city which the Book of Revelation later mentions symbolically. Some early commentators (e.g. Ticonius and St Bede) saw the two witnesses as standing for the Old and New Testaments; but this interpretation has had little following. St Jerome (Epist. 59) say that they are Elijah and Enoch, and St Gregory the Great and others give that interpretation (Moralia, 9,4).

What St John is doing is using a theme which occurs fairly frequently in apocalyptic writings where Elijah and Enoch or other combinations of prominent figures are portrayed as opponents of antichrist. His two witnesses do have features of Elijah and Moses, both of whom bore witness to Christ at the Transfiguration (cf Mt 17:1-8 and par.). However, the duration of the trial they undergo, and the entire context of the passage, point rather to them standing for the prophetic witness of the Church, symbolized by certain more outstanding witnesses, who were present at the death of Christ, which took place in Jerusalem, and who were also witnesses of his glorious resurrection. However, it is the entire Church, right through the course of its history, that has been given the prophetic role of calling men to repentance in the midst of harassment and hostility: "The holy People of God shares also in Christ's prophetic office: it spreads a broad and living witness to him, especially by a life of faith and love and by offering to God a sacrifice of praise, the fruit of lips praising his name (cf. Heb 13:15)" (Vatican II, Lumen gentium, 12). "The Church announces the good tidings of salvation […], so that all men may believe the one true God and Jesus Christ whom he has sent and may be converted from their ways, doing penance (cf. Jn 17:3; Lk 24:27; Acts 2:38)" (Vatican II Sacrosanctum Concilium, 9).

7-10 The prophet Daniel used four beasts to symbolize the empires of the world as enemies of the people of Israel. In the Apocalypse the beast stands for the enemy of the Church and the enemy of god. Further on it will develop this theme and link the beasts to the dragon or satan (cf. 13:2), and describe their defeat by Christ, the Lamb of God (cf. 14:1; 19:19-21).

The symbol of the beast is brought forward in this passage to show that there will be a point, or various points, before the End when the forces of evil will apparently win victory. Martyrdom silences the voices of the witnesses of Jesus Christ who preach repentance; many will rejoice over this and even deride those whose words or actions they find uncomfortable, despite the fact that when a Christian bears witness to the salvation that comes from Jesus he is motivated purely by love. "Since Jesus, the Son of God, showed his love by laying down his life for us, no one has greater love than he who lays down his life for him and for his brothers (cf. 1 Jn 3:16; Jn 15:13). Some Christians have been called from the beginning, and will always be called, to give this greatest testimony of love to all, especially to persecutors. Martyrdom makes the disciple like his Master, who willingly accepted death for the salvation of the world, and through it he is conformed to Him by the shedding of blood. Therefore the Church considers it the highest gift and supreme test of love. And while it is given to few, all however must be prepared to confess Christ before men and to follow him along the way of the cross amidst the persecutions which the Church never lacks" (Lumen gentium, 42).

"The great city", whose name is not given, seems to be Jerusalem, which in Isaiah 1:10 is called Sodom because it has turned its back on God. However, when the writer tells us that it is "allegorically called Sodom and Egypt, where their Lord was crucified" (v. 8), we may take Jerusalem here to stand for any city or even any nation where perversity holds sway (cf. Wis 19:14-17, which alludes to Sodom and Egypt) and where Christians are persecuted and hunted down (cf. Acts 9:5). Thus, St Jerome (Epist. 17) interpreted the names of Sodom and Egypt as having a mystical or figurative meaning, referring to the entire world seen as the city of the devil and of evildoers.

Further on, St John will identify the Rome of his time with the "great city" (cf. 17:9). Evil will triumph for only a limited period. Its reign is fixed to last "three days and a half", to show its brevity and temporary character as compared with the one thousand two hundred and sixty day (three years and a half) for which the prophetic witness endures (cf. note on 11:1-2).

11-13 Those who have given their lives to bear witness to Jesus will also, through the power of the Holy Spirit, share in his resurrection and ascension into heaven. The writer describes this by various references to the Old Testament, references rich in meaning. The breath of life which causes the witnesses to stand up, that is, to be resurrected, reveals the power of the Spirit of God, which is also described by the prophet Ezekiel in his vision of the dry bones which become living warriors (cf. Ezek 37:1-14). The voice which calls them up to heaven reminds us of what happed to Elijah at the end of his life (cf 2 Kings 2:11) and to certain other Old testament saints like Enoch (cf Gen 5:24; Sir 44:16); according to certain Jewish traditions (cf. Flavius Josephus, Jewish Antiquities, IV, 8, 48), all of these men were carried up into heaven at the end of their days on earth.

The exaltation of the witnesses is in sharp contrast with the punishment meted out to their enemies, a punishment designed to move men to conversion. The earthquake indicates that the chastisement is sudden and unexpected; the number of those who die symbolizes a great crowd (thousands) embracing all types (seven).

The prophecy of the two witnesses is a call to the Christian to bear witness to Christ in the midst of persecution, even to the point of martyrdom. It makes it quite clear that God does not abandon those who boldly take his side. If the prophets of the Old Testament suffered martyrdom, the same will happen in the new, only more so: the messianic times have begun, persecution will grow in strength, but the end of the world is approaching.

14 The tribulations connected with the blowing of the last three trumpets are thrown into sharp and terrible relief by the three "woes" announced from heaven (cf. 8:13), which are a kind of loud lamentation. The second "woe" has been described as something that has already taken place, and the third one is announced. Thus, after the parenthesis of 10:1 – 11:13, the thread of the narrative (following the successive trumpet blasts) is taken up again, and our attention is drawn to the importance of what follows.

15 The seventh trumpet opens a new section which will tell us, about the climax of the confrontation between Satan and the powers of evil, and Christ and the Church (cf 12:1 – 16:16), and then go on to describe the last battles, with Christ triumphing as Lord of all forever (cf 16:17 – 22:5). All this is prefaced by an introduction which tells us that his kingdom will come and will endure forever.

The description of the confrontation between Christ and Satan begins with the war between the dragon and the beasts, on the one hand, and the Messiah, the woman and her children, on the other (cf 12:1 – 13:18). Then the Lamb appears. Christ in glory, and the moment of judgment is announced (cf 14:1-20). This is depicted by the seven bowls or plagues (cf 15:1 – 16:16); when the seventh plague is released, the contenders are introduced again, and the account of the last battles follows (cf 16:17).

As announced earlier (cf 10:17), the bowling of the seventh trumpet means that God's mysterious design has been fully implemented. The voices from heaven (11:15) proclaim the revelation of this mystery: that divine design which makes Christ reign forever has taken effect. As elsewhere in the New Testament (cf Acts 4:25-28), this passage of the Apocalypse also teaches that Christ's complete dominion fulfils the prophetic words of Psalm 2. The climax of human history is the full installation of Christ's Kingdom; the Apocalypse, given its perspective, views this as a present event. It thereby offers Christians a great message of hope and consolation, for the Church "is on earth the seed and the beginning of that kingdom. While it slowly grows to maturity, the Church longs for the complete kingdom and, with all its strength, hopes and desires to be united in glory with its king" (Vatican II, Lumen gentium, 5).

Jesus himself teaches us to pray constantly to the Father. "Thy Kingdom com."

16-18 In response to this revelation from God, his people (represented by the twenty-four elders: cf. 4:4) hasten to adore him and thank him. Although all this is placed in a celestial context, it also represents the Church's response to its Redeemer's victorious struggle, which will culminate in his second coming. At that point almighty God will establish his absolute sovereignty; that period will come to an end in which God in his infinite patience permitted man to rebel against him; and all men who ever existed will be judged. This is the faith the Church professes when it proclaims its belief in Jesus Christ, "who will come again in glory to judge the living and the dead" (Nicene-Constantinopolitan Creed).

The author of the Apocalypse carries us forward to that final moment when God's action in human history reaches its climax. That is why it no longer speaks of God with reference to the future (as it previously did)—he "who is and who was and who is to come": cf. Rev 1:4, 8, 4:8 — but rather in relation to the present and the past—"who art and who wast" (v. 17).

At this final point in history God's justice is fully revealed. Insofar as it involves the condemnation of those who oppose him it is referred to as his "anger" or "wrath" (cf. Rom 1:18). Only God has the power to establish enduring justice or righteousness, as Psalms 96 and 98 tell us.

Mankind is divided into two groups—those who are rewarded and those who are destroyed; cf. how our Lord describes the Last Judgment in Matthew 25:31-46. The first group consists of those who, down the centuries (in the times of both the Old and New Covenants) have borne witness to Christ (the prophets), those who have been sanctified by Baptism and have striven for holiness (the saints), and all people great and small who have sought God with sincerity of heart. The second group consists of those who have not kept the law of God (impressed on Creation itself) and who by their sins have helped to corrupt the world by serving the powers of evil (cf. Rev 19:2). When it says that God will destroy them that does not mean that he will annihilate them but rather that he will make them incapable of doing any more evil and will punish them as they deserve. On the Last Judgment, see the notes on Matthew 25:31-46.

19 The seer introduces the heavenly temple (the location par excellence of God's presence), paralleling the earlier mention of the temple of Jerusalem (cf. 11:1-2). The opening of the temple and the sight of the Ark of the Covenant show that the messianic era has come to an end and God's work of salvation has been completed. The ark was the symbol of Israel's election and salvation and of God's presence in the midst of his people. According to a Jewish tradition, reported in 2 Maccabees 2: 4-8, Jeremiah placed the ark in a secret hiding place prior to the destruction of Jerusalem, and it would be seen again when the Messiah came. The author of the Apocalypse uses this to assure us that God has not forgotten his covenant: he has sealed it definitively in heaven, where the arc is located.

Many early commentators interpreted the ark as a reference to Christ's sacred humanity, and St Bede explains that just as the manna was kept in the original ark, so Christ's divinity lies hidden in his sacred body (cf. Explanatio Apocalypsis, 11, 19).

The heavenly covenant is the new and eternal one made by Jesus Christ (cf. Mt 26:26-29 and par.) which will be revealed to all at his second coming when the Church will triumph, as the Apocalypse goes on to describe. The presence of the ark in the heavenly temple symbolizes the sublimity of the messianic kingdom, which exceeds anything man could create. "The vigilant and active expectation of the coming of the Kingdom is also the expectation of a finally perfect justice for the living and the dead, for people of all times and places, a justice which Jesus Christ, installed as supreme Judge, will establish (cf. Mt 24:29-44, 46; Acts 10:42, 2 Cor 5:10). This promise, which surpasses all human possibilities, directly concerns our life in this world. For true justice must include everyone; it must explain the immense load of suffering borne by all generations. In fact, without the resurrection of the dead and the Lord's judgment, there is no justice in the full sense of the term. The promise of the resurrection is freely made to meet the desire for true justice dwelling in the human heart" (SCDF, Libertatis conscientia, 60).

The thunder and lightning which accompany the appearance of the ark are reminiscent of the way God made his presence felt on Sinai; they reveal God's mighty intervention (cf. Rev 4:5; 8:5) which is now accompanied by the chastisement Hearing the Trumpet Sounds.

CHAPTER 8
OUR LADY OF REVELATIONS

We now we have an actual photograph of Blessed Virgin Mary. This is for the description of what we will now title "Our Lady of Revelations". This is the pictorial representation, proof, of St. John's Gospel. Revelations 12:1-4, he states 1 "And a great sign appeared in the heaven: a woman clothed with the sun, and the moon was under her feet, and upon her head a crown of twelve stars."

There is an actual photograph of the Blessed Virgin Mary taken in a major apparition to Father David, a miracle-working Capuchin priest. He has the wounds of the stigmata, of the crucifixion of Jesus Christ, confirmed by the Pope John Paul II and His Vatican Doctor.

Blessed Mother appears to Father David often. Padre Pio appears to Father David very often. Other saints have appeared to Father too. For now, we are speaking about this one major apparition. Father was walking in a very holy, wooded area in his country. He was walking with his seminarians, and Blessed Mother appeared to him. Her image, when she appeared, was extremely striking. They happened to have a small camera with them because they were looking for land to expand their orphanages. That is why they were in a beautiful wooded area which is prime for that space. When Blessed Mothers appears, he often asks permission to take a photograph of her, and Blessed Mother gives permission. Once Blessed Mother gives permission, he then takes the photograph of the Blessed Virgin Mary. I have several images of these, up to 10 of these photographs of Blessed Mother during this apparition

Father was walking through a wooded area. There were several seminarians with Father. Father is a Capuchin monk, a priest. And Blessed Mother appeared to him in an extremely large image. Father's camera is not a professional camera. It is a little digital camera with discs. When I was with Father David, about a year ago, he showed me these most startling photographs. He explained that Blessed Mother appeared in this apparition over 20 feet tall. The actual apparition is that Blessed Mother is standing on top of the globe, on the earth. We can see mountain ranges and water, high and low, depicting what the astronauts would have seen several hundred miles in the air. They would see the globe, the earth in this way. So we see dark brown mountain ranges, blue mountain ranges; in other words, it is showing higher and lower elevations. We also see a dark blue under her feet, which is depicting the oceans. So she is standing on top of the earth. It is clearly the earth. This is a real, real photograph of Blessed Mother.

I spoke to Father at least 12 times over several months, each time asking for the release of this picture. Would Blessed Mother allow it to be shown to the public? The photograph is the most striking in the world. It is (I can't emphasize this enough), a real, real, real photograph of the Blessed Virgin Mary; the only one in the history of the world.

So the first question comes: Why would the Blessed Mother allow a photograph of this apparition when they did not take any in Medjugorje, which is one of the most recent apparitions, or other recent apparitions, (Medjugorje being the most famous). The six visionaries never asked to take a photograph of Blessed Virgin Mary. It never occurred to them, they never asked it, and, therefore, it was never done. Likely, permission would not have been granted. So, as real as Medjugorje could be (it is not yet approved by the Catholic Church), it never came into their minds to take a picture of Blessed Mother in Medjugorje, on Apparition Hill, or wherever she appears regularly to them. And she appeared for decades, more than 30 years now. And still, there is no photograph. There is no photograph of any other apparitions of Blessed Virgin Mary in the world. That means that this is the only photograph of an actual apparition of the Blessed Virgin Mary in the world. It is REAL. You will see it immediately as: This is a real picture! This also is the most beautiful, beautiful woman I have ever seen in my life! You will be awestruck and shocked to see this.

We are not able to show you the photograph now, Blessed Mother repeatedly forbade the release of this photograph. She sees Father David regularly. He sees her. He talks to her. She speaks to Father also. Blessed Mother said she will let Father David know when this picture can be released to the world. As a result, we are waiting for that.

As a explanation about photograph, I am going to describe the picture of Blessed Mother, as it is here. I have several photographs that Father took in different angles of the Blessed Virgin Mary. So, while I am not showing it, I am going to describe it. The reason for the description of this is because of the major apparition that Father had on December 20th of last year, 2013. Blessed Mother told the actual dates of the very beginning of the tribulation, and the chastisement, and the judgment, and so on. Because of its timing, the world is not ready to see the photograph. That is what this book is all about. Now, there is likely, possibly very likely, to be earthquakes all over the world. And earthquakes cause tsunamis, and they cause disasters, all over the world.

Now, getting back to this photograph, Blessed Mother does not want this released anywhere. She strictly forbade it being shown. However, it is likely that she will, (according to what Father is surmising) be likely to give permission after the July chastisement, July 4th to July 27 and beyond. We are praying for the mitigation of that, the lessening of that. Nevertheless, permission would, in my opinion (Francis Slinsky) be given then. There is a reason for giving permission then. She doesn't want this to be released untimely. She wants it to be a soothing, comforting sign from Jesus and the Blessed Mother, that she is going to bring peace throughout the world after the chastisement. That is what this image actually depicts.

I want to describe the picture itself now. According to Father, and he is from Italy, therefore, I have to clarify everything he says several times to make sure I am one hundred percent correct about what he is saying. Not only do I ask essentially the same question several times from different approaches, different angles, or different words, but I also have asked him about this for the last year since I saw it.

He happened to fly into California once. And I flew out there. He took his disc from his camera and went to a CVS pharmacy store. We made copies, actual photographs of this on a photo-printer. The manager was there, and it just shocked this woman manager completely. We have a hundred -percent assurance that there are no copies in the CVS printer. Therefore, when we did the print at CVS and we have the only copies. That is imperative. There are several pictures, several angles, so I picked out the best one to describe. Hopefully, when Blessed Mother gives permission to release this we will be able to get this out very specially, globally, on YouTube, Internet and every other media in the world then at that time.

The description of the photograph is this: Blessed Mother is standing on the top of the earth, the globe, as mentioned. She is standing on a continent where there are mountain ranges. There are different colors, so you can see there are different heights. There is also a darker blue, which depicts the oceans. Her bare feet are firmly planted on the earth. Revelations 1 St. John's gospel: A sign will appear in the heavens. Behind Blessed Mother are the heavens. When Father took this picture, I asked him how tall was Blessed Mother, because her feet appear to be bigger than her face. (Whatever is more distant becomes smaller, according to the perspective of the camera in a photo.) This is proof that Blessed Mother's image was enormous in size in the apparition. According to Father the image of Blessed Mother alone is over 20 feet tall. More than a two-story building. She is already over 20 feet high. The earth is under her and above her there is the cloud formation of a dove symbolizing the Holy Spirit and twelve Hebrew stars. So the actual image is somewhere in the vicinity of 27 feet high or more. Enormous! So Father asked Blessed Mother, he said, "I have a little camera. Can I take this?" He took the photograph of her in four stages. He took a photo of her feet first. Then he took the middle of Blessed Mother. Then he took Blessed Mother's face and shoulders. Then he took above Blessed Mother. It's actually in four parts. Then he stood back and took the entire photograph.

Now, for the description. Blessed Mother's feet: these are real feet. You will know "Wow! That's real flesh, real feet, real skin!" What else is real, is Blessed Mother's face is the most beautiful, most life-like, most beautiful image of any woman in the world. So you have the most beautiful image of Blessed Mother, her face. Her face, her hair which is coming down over her shoulders is real. You will notice and say immediately, "That's real hair, that's real skin, that's really the face, that's really the feet of a woman, therefore Blessed Mother. And that's really the hands of Blessed Mother. However, it ends there. Her beautiful blue mantle is soft silk-like, not in sharp focus. Now Father's camera was a very inexpensive camera, and yet he was able to capture the exquisite detail; in the face, the eyes, the eyelids, eye lashes, and everything is exactly perfect as if you had a very good camera, and it's able to focus on a particular part of a very large image. It will bring that part of the image into extremely sharp detail. The rest of it will be blurrier. Some of it will be very blurry. Because you're only focusing on one part of what is likely a 25 foot tall image right in front of you. The fact that her gown is out of focus, soft, touchable, cuddly, if you will, is another miracle. Because you're saying Wow! That is so real. That is so soft. But it's not sharp. That is to say, the face and the hands and the feet and the hair are real. That's all that's real. The rest of it, her beautiful gown and mantle and veil are slightly unfocused.

In the photograph Blessed Mother is looking down on the earth. You may have seen similar pictures of the Blessed Virgin like this before. It is like the Lady of the Miraculous Medal, or Our Lady of Grace. There are artist's representations of this image of Blessed Mother but without the heavens, without the Holy Spirit. You will say, "Oh, I've seen that picture before." You haven't!! Because in Blessed Mother's hands the rays are coming right out of her palms, not out of rings. In the Miraculous Medal, the rays, the graces were coming out of the rings, out of the back of her hands. These rays are coming straight out of her palms. You can see the rays pouring out of her palms. It is not photo-shopped, it's real! The second thing you will notice is that there are 12 perfectly- formed Hebrew stars (the six-pointed stars) around her head. The crescent moon is under her robe. So I am going to go over it again. You are going to see the twelve stars around her head, you are going to see the rays coming out of her palms, the crescent moon under her robe, and a great sign appearing in the heavens. You can see a tremendous amount of the sky in this photo. One of the most striking parts is that there is an ominous, horrendous, startling, scary, blackened sky as if right after a tornado or after a hurricane without the rain. The darkened sky is scary. But in the middle of the darkened sky (which is the chastisement) is bright sunlight behind and on Blessed Mother. You can see that the sun is on her. The image directly over her head is the Holy Spirit. You will see the left and right wings of the Holy Spirit, in a cloud-like formation. In the Bible it says "The Holy Spirit will come upon you." Here the Holy Spirit is upon Mary. He is over her head.

I think I have described enough of the picture. What you have is the darkened sky, you have the lightened sky, (clouds where the sun is hitting on it). You have the cloud formation of the Holy Spirit because you can see the wings and they are over Blessed Mother. You clearly can see that the rays are coming out of Blessed Mother's palms, you clearly can see that the crescent moon is under her robe, that the globe is real. Her hands are real, her hair is real, her feet are real. And the fact that, in perspective, her feet appear larger than her face, shows the tall size of the image. It is an exquisite photograph that everybody should have. I don't know for certain that it will be shown, but if and when Blessed Mother gives Father David permission to show this picture, I am going to humbly ask Father (and I am the least worthy) but will ask humbly, would Blessed Mother bless every copy of the photograph that people receive. Since this is a holy picture, I am going to ask that Blessed Mother to then bless every one of these herself as a further protection that people can hang this on their wall. So it will be blessed by Blessed Mother, a most striking picture. At this juncture, that is all that I can say about this. We are writing this information now, putting it in the book. We are going to do the best we can. I have no further information. I cannot give any further description, nor can I release this picture.

When and if Blessed Mother gives permission for the photograph to be shown to the world, we will have it on our website at Marysway.net.

CHAPTER 9
ALL-IMPORTANT FACTS ABOUT
MARY'S WAY APOSTOLATE

Mary's Way to Jesus Worldwide Apostolate, Inc. is a dynamic Worldwide Apostolate devoted to Jesus through His Most Holy Mother Mary. An "Apostolate" is a group of people working together to promote a Doctrine of the Catholic Church which is "Our Lady Mediatrix of All Graces"! *Mary's Way* has been operating for 16 years. Its Founder and Director is Francis Slinsky. Please contact us at www.marysway.net or by phone 1-732-892-7400 or by mail at: Mary's Way Worldwide Apostolate, 990 Cedar Bridge Avenue, Suite B7-150, Brick, New Jersey 08723 USA.

Mary's Way to Jesus Apostolate began in Mary's month in May 1996, when Marie Tully, a very devout woman, received three very clear inner locutions from Jesus during "Exposition of the Blessed Sacrament" *IN SAINT JOHN THE BAPTIST CATHOLIC CHURCH* in New York City. Jesus asked Marie to "go to Medjugorje to go see my Mother." Marie quickly went to Medjugorje and to her surprise, she arrived in Medjugorje on *"THE FEAST DAY OF SAINT JOHN THE BAPTIST"*, June 24, 1996, which was also "The 15th Anniversary of the ongoing Apparitions in Medjugorje".

Marie met with Vicka (Medjugorje) the highly spirited Visionary of Mary that day! That evening, during an apparition of the Blessed Virgin Mary in Medjugorje, Vicka held up Rosary Beads and Brown Scapulars including those of Marie's friend in the United States, Francis Slinsky. The Blessed Virgin Mary blessed Francis' Rosary and Brown Scapular in the evening of "The Feast Day of Saint John the Baptist" in Medjugorje!

During the night, of *"The Feast Day of Saint John the Baptist"*, *Saint Louis de Montfort, the most Marian of all saints,* appeared to Francis in a dream in the United States. In the dream, Saint Louis was wearing his very distinct 17th. century priest habit. Saint Louis de Montfort came down the aisle from the altar after Mass in a church *named in honor of Saint Dominic* to whom our Lady said: *"One day through the Rosary and the Scapular she would save the world"*. In the dream, Saint Louis accurately foretold the creation and coming of the unique Sacred Icon *"Our Lady Mediatrix of All Graces"* to Francis who would surprisingly, soon become this Sacred Icon's caretaker.

Four weeks later on a Saturday *dedicated to the Blessed Virgin Mary* , July 26th, on *"THE FEAST DAY OF SAINT ANN AND SAINT JOACHIM"*, *the Blessed Mother's Mother and Father,* Francis (who had been looking through dozens of picture books of Saints for a month to find out who the saint was that appeared in the dream) conclusively confirmed through pictorial comparisons that it was indeed Saint Louis de Montfort in the dream, with the same face, the same facial features, and the same stature, wearing the same very distinct 17th century priestly habit!

Exactly 73 days later (there are 73 Books in the Bible), on October 7th, on *"THE FEAST DAY OF OUR LADY OF THE ROSARY"* the last two parts, of the 3-Part Purpose of "Our Lady Mediatrix of All Graces" Sacred Icon, was foretold in a profound second dream to Francis which is: *WHOEVER VENERATES MARY THROUGH HER MOST POWERFUL ROLE AS "MEDIATRIX OF ALL GRACES" WILL RECEIVE (1) VAST OUTPOURINGS OF ALL OF GOD'S GRACES, (2) PROTECTION AGAINST ALL EVIL, (3) AND COMPLETE LASTING PEACE!*

In retrospect, many spiritually significant events and dates are linked to the creation of "Our Lady Mediatrix of All Graces" Miraculous Icon. For example, on *"THE FEAST DAY OF THE MOTHERHOOD OF THE BLESSED VIRGIN MARY"*, Mary's Way Apostolate was established. Two days later, on October 13th, 1996, on *"THE ANNIVERSARY OF THE GREAT MIRACLE OF THE SUN IN FATIMA"*, Josyp Terelya from the Ukraine, one of the world's finest Icon painters (writers), mystic, and world renowned Marian Visionary offered to paint the Icon *WITH MARY'S TRUE HEAVENLY FACE* – most surprisingly, *DURING A SAINT LOUIS DE MONTFORT RELIGIOUS CONFERENCE!* It was Saint Louis De Montfort who appeared in the dream to Francis and foretold the Icon's coming!

On November 13 and on December 13, through inspiration, vitally important additions were made to the Icon. THE ICON WAS COMPLETED ON "CHRISTMAS DAY" 1996 – *"AS MARY'S GIFT TO THE ENTIRE WORLD"* GIVEN TO EVERYONE ON THE 2000th BIRTHDAY OF JESUS!" (There is a 4 year error in our calendars. It occurred when our present "Gregorian Calendar" was revised in the year 1582 from "The Julian Calendar".)

Chapter 10

*FORTY VITALLY IMPORTANT FACTS AND DATES ABOUT
THE MIRACULOUS ICON ®
OUR LADY MEDIATRIX OF ALL GRACES ®*

1. Seemingly miraculous, our Blessed Mother's eyes in "The Miraculous Icon" are always looking directly at you - where ever you move, her loving eyes are always following you, she is always looking after you, she never leaves you, her beloved child! If you look at the Icon on the Wall while standing in the center of it - Our Lady is of course looking directly at you. When you move to the extreme right or the extreme left of the Icon are Lady's eyes will follow you wherever you move and will still be looking directly at you! Even if your back is flat against the wall on the left or right our Blessed Mother is always looking directly at you!

2. Blessed Mother's face in "Our Lady Mediatrix of All Graces" Miraculous Icon is the alleged true face of Mary, the Mother of God, the same face Saint Luke the Evangelist painted on an Icon of her while she was in Saint John the Apostle's Home in Ephesus. The Icon that Saint Luke painted is almost 2,000 years old, and venerated in Saint Mary Major Papal Basilica in Rome, Italy. It is the only Icon of Mary in the Papal Basilicas.

3. It is the only Icon of "Our Lady Mediatrix of All Graces" in the world! This was documented by the world's largest Marian Library which has over 22,000 images of Mary: The International Marian Library at Dayton Ohio in the United States which is directly linked to the Vatican Library in Rome. It was interiorly arranged and designed by Our Lady for the vitally important upcoming Dogma: "Our Lady Mediatrix of All Graces,..."!

4. This Sacred Icon has an astonishing 545 Iconic details! Some of the most important details that are in the Icon are that it has: All Four Marian Dogmas, The First Dogma "THE MOTHER OF GOD", The Second Dogma "PERPETUAL VIRGINITY", The Third Dogma "THE IMMACULATE CONCEPTION", The Fourth Dogma "THE ASSUMPTION"; the proposed 3-part Final Marian Dogma: "OUR LADY MEDIATRIX OF ALL GRACES"®, "COREDEMPTRIX", "ADVOCATE"; all 7 of the most important stages of Mary's life: "THE ANNUNCIATION", "THE VISITATION", "THE NATIVITY", "THE PRESENTATION", "THE FINDING IN THE TEMPLE", "THE WEDDING AT CANA", "THE CRUCIFIXION"; every vital part of Mary's life: "THE NEW EVE", "THE NEW ADAM", "THE WOMAN OF REVELATIONS", etc. See History – Article 15 in our website for complete details.

5. All of the 13 features in "Mary's beautiful Heavenly Face: on Our Lady Mediatrix of All Graces® Icon at Mary's Way Apostolate are identical to, and are fully corroborated by, the independently written descriptions that were given many years earlier by all six Medjugorje Visionaries! They each independently, twice gave their written descriptions to their spiritual director who wrote about them in his writings and about "Mary's Heavenly Face", including the most important feature, that MARY HAS A LIGHT COLOR BROW!

6. These six Visionaries had each seen "Mary's Heavenly Face" hundreds of

times for many years! MARY'S "LIGHT COLOR BROW" IS: THE DOVE OF THE HOLY SPIRIT INDELIBLY AGLOW ON MARY'S BROW IN HEAVEN, and also subtly shown on The Miraculous Icon - Our Lady Mediatrix of All Graces! This further, definitively shows that the Sacred Miraculous Icon has the alleged « true, real Heavenly Face of Mary ».

7. The Icon was very specially painted by Josyp Terelya, world renowned mystic and Marian visionary, chosen by Our Lady and the only person who could paint this Icon accurately!

8. So many Favors, Graces and Blessings, Healings and over 200 Miracles have been mediated by Mary. Our Lady also arranged and directed that her Sacred Icon be in a private audience with Pope John Paul II along with Francis Slinsky, the Founder and Director of Mary's Way to Jesus Worldwide Apostolate. This Icon is now known worldwide as The Miraculous Icon®. See TESTIMONIALS in our website for complete details.

9. ON "THE FEAST DAY OF SAINT JOHN THE BAPTIST" June 24, 1996, the Sacred Icon was foretold to Francis, in a dream by Saint Louis de Montfort!

10. ON "THE FEAST DAY OF SAINT ANN AND SAINT JOACHIM" the Blessed Mother's Mother and Father June 26, 1996, on a Saturday dedicated to the Blessed Virgin Mary, Francis, looking through dozens of picture books of Saints for a month, found conclusively that the Saint who appeared in the dream, WAS SAINT LOUIS DE MONTFORT the most Marian of all saints!

11. ON "THE FEAST DAY OF THE HOLY ROSARY" October 7, 1996 THE LAST 2 PARTS, OF THE 3-PART PURPOSE OF "OUR LADY MEDIATRIX OF ALL GRACES" SACRED ICON, WAS FORETOLD IN A PROFOUND SECOND DREAM to Francis which is: whoever venerates Mary through her Most Powerful Role as "Mediatrix of All Graces" WILL RECEIVE (1) VAST OUTPOURINGS OF ALL OF GOD'S GRACES, (2) PROTECTION AGAINST ALL EVIL, and (3) COMPLETE LASTING PEACE!

12. ON "THE FEAST DAY OF MARY, MOTHER OF THE CHURCH" October 11, 1996, MARY'S WAY WORLDWIDE APOSTOLATE, INC. WAS OFFICIALLY, FORMALLY ESTABLISHED as a New Jersey establishment.

13. ON "THE FEAST DAY OF THE GREAT MIRACLE OF FATIMA" October 13, 1996, Francis Slinsky very surprisingly commissioned Josyp Terelya to paint the Icon at a Saint Louis de Montfort Religious Conference. The religious conference was entitled "True Devotion to Mary", "The Twin Pillars of Victory" from the well-known Prophetic Dream of Saint John Bosco. The two pillars to which The Catholic Church is anchored to in times of trouble are: The Eucharist, and Our Lady!

14. Through Inspiration, on November 13, 1996 the Icon has to be completely

repainted to Iconically paint "The Wedding Feast of Cana" and "The Crucifixion" in the upper left corner and the upper right corner of the Icon and the "Ichthus" on the bottom middle of the Icon.

15. Again through Inspiration, on December 13, 1996 the Sacred Icon had to be completely repainted to add the Icon's Title in Latin DOMINA NOSTRA MEDIATRIX OMNIUM GRATIARUM (Our Lady Mediatrix of All Graces) in a banner around Mary's head.

16. ON "CHRISTMAS DAY" December 25, 1996, The Miraculous Icon of Lady Mediatrix of All Graces was completed by Josyp Terelya. IT IS OUR BLESSED MOTHER'S SPECIAL GIFT, HER CHRISTMAS PRESENT TO THE ENTIRE WORLD!

17. ON "THE FEAST DAY OF THE SOLEMNITY OF MARY, MOTHER OF GOD" January 1, 1997, the Icon was solemnly blessed by Bishop Roman Danylak at Mass in Canada in The Eastern Holy Roman Catholic Church, Ukrainian Rite.

18. The Icon was shipped on February 13, 1997 by Josyp Terelya from Toronto, Canada to Mary's Way in the United States.

19. ON "SAINT VALENTINE'S DAY" February 14, 1997, the Icon arrived from Toronto, Canada - where Josyp Terelya lived and where he painted this Sacred Icon - into the United States. The large box in which the Original Miraculous Icon was shipped is Dated and Time Stamped (in military time) crossing the Canadian border into the United States AT EXACTLY, ON THE FIRST 13th MINUTE of Valentine's Day "STAMPED 00.13 – which is also the number related to "Our Lady of Fatima"! This was Our Lady's "Stamp of Approval", her "Token of Love" for all! "The Miraculous Icon", "Our Lady Mediatrix of All Graces" is somehow mysteriously linked to "Our Lady of Fatima", and to "Our Lady of Medjugorje" (1917, 1981, 1996).

20. THROUGHOUT THE LAST 16 YEARS, THE CARETAKER OF "THE MIRACULOUS ICON" "OUR LADY MEDIATRIX OF ALL GRACES" WAS GIVEN OVER 2,000 VISIBLE SIGNS OF "THE NUMBER 13" WHICH IS OUR LADY'S WAY OF PERFECTLY GUIDING HIM, ASSURING HIM, AND CONFIRMING TO HIM - HOW EXTREMELY IMPORTANT "OUR LADY MEDIATRIX OF ALL GRACES" IS FOR EVERYONE IN THE WORLD!

21. When the Sacred Icon arrived at "Mary's Way to Jesus Apostolate", a single blessed 7-day candle was lit for the Icon of "Our Lady Mediatrix of All Graces", and also for "Our Lady of Fatima", and for "Our Lady of Medjugorje" which are all very mysteriously linked to the Sacred Icon "Our Lady Mediatrix of All Graces"! After 4 days of burning, the votive candle, with 3 days of candle wax still left, BURNED "MIRACULOUSLY" FOR EXACTLY 3 HOURS: FOR JESUS' 3 HOURS ON THE CROSS! (I showed my wife: that the time was from

EXACTLY 1:13 TO 4:13 AGAIN THE SIGNS 13!)

22. The burning candle wick on the blessed votive candle split apart, and the top half of the burning, split candle wick then slowly TURNED INTO THE SHAPE OF A PERFECT CRUCIFIX and it is still at the bottom of the saved 12 inch glass cylinder which held the 7 day votive altar candle!

23. In addition, the top of the split burning candle wick curled into the shape of a perfect Paschal-shaped letter "P" REPRESENTING THE SACRIFICIAL, PASCHAL LAMB ON THE ALTAR OF THE CROSS – at the top of "The burning Candle Wick Crucifix"! This was videotaped and shown to others.

24. Also miraculously, when the candle burned out, the remains of the burnt, blackened candle wick – TURNED WHITE, AND THEN TURNED INTO THE OUTLINE OF A PERFECT "ICHTHYS" (a fish symbolizing all Christians – "a sign" that this is the Icon for all Christians throughout the world) at the bottom of the 8 inch glass container which held the candle – and is still there! THE EXACT SAME WHITE-OUTLINED "ICHTHYS" IS PAINTED ON THE MIRACULOUS ICON®, ALSO AT THE BOTTOM! After burning hundreds of candles this has never happened again!

25. ON "THE FEAST DAY OF THE ANNUNCIATION" March 25, 1997, the Original Icon of "Our Lady Mediatrix of All Graces" was most powerfully and most solemnly blessed at the Altar at Mass in the Eastern Roman Catholic Byzantine Rite by Reverend Konstantine Brown in Saint Mary's of the Assumption Byzantine Catholic Church, Trenton, New Jersey. This was the very first blessing of the Original Miraculous Icon, Our Lady Mediatrix of All Graces. This most powerful, most solemn "All Healing and an All Evil Dispelling Blessing" Prayer has since then been used on all of our Icons and religious articles.

26. The Sacred Icon of Our Lady Mediatrix of All Graces® of Child Jesus and Mary went "mysteriously missing for 3 days" in Rome from May 28 to May 31, 1997 while on a pilgrimage to a religious conference! This parallels the event in the Bible, where Child Jesus went "mysteriously missing for 3 days" on a pilgrimage and a religious conference! It was found 3 days later through much prayer and through the help of the Italian Government Minister of Art, the International President of Vox Populi Mariae Mediatrici Dr. Mark Miravalle, Archbishops and Bishops, and members of the International Catholic movement "Voice of the People for Mary Mediatrix"!

27. ON "THE FEAST DAY OF THE VISITATION" May 31, 1997, the Icon's very first blessing in the Roman Catholic Church was by his Eminence Alphonse Cardinal Stickler the Librarian and Archivist of the entire Holy Roman Catholic Church in Rome, Italy - in a solemn High Mass concelebrated with Cardinal Martinez, together with 13 Archbishops, 42 Bishops, and 25 Priests - 80 on the Altar from 40 different Countries from around the world!

Our Lady arranged and designed that The Original Mary Mediatrix Icon was blessed in The Church of The House of Mary on May 31, 1997, the Feast of "The Visitation".

28. The Original Icon of "Our Lady Mediatrix of All Graces" was on stage and honored throughout the entire "Vox Populi Mariae Mediatrici 1997 International Conference" in Rome from May 30 through June 2, 1997. In attendance were Cardinals, Archbishops, Bishops, Priests, internationally renowned theologians and Marian leaders from 55 countries!

29. On May 30, 1998, "Our Lady Mediatrix of All Graces" also arranged that her Icon was very specially honored by being on the Altar in "The Church of the House of Mary" in a solemn High Mass concelebrated by the Pope's Curia Cardinal, his Eminence Alphonse Cardinal Stickler with 110 Archbishops, Bishops, and Priests, on the altar from 70 Different Countries!

30. On May 29 through May 31, 1998, the Original Icon of "Our Lady Mediatrix of All Graces" was on stage and honored throughout the entire "Vox Populi Mariae Mediatrici" "1998 International Leadership Conference" in Rome.

31. ON "THE ORIGINAL FEAST DAY OF 'OUR LADY MEDIATRIX OF ALL GRACES'", WHICH WAS ALSO "THE FEAST OF THE VISITATION" May 31, 1998, THE ORIGINAL ICON WAS PLACED ON A SPECIAL EASEL IN SAINT PETER'S BASILICA NEXT TO MICHELANGELO'S PIETA! THE ORIGINAL MEDIATRIX ICON was mysteriously, so very wonderfully kept next to Michelangelo's Pietà in Saint Peter's Basilica FOR EXACTLY 33 HOURS – allegedly FOR JESUS' 33 YEARS ON EARTH! This parallels the event in the Bible, where Jesus was on earth for 33 years, represented by the 33 hours!

32. On May 12, 1999, Our Lady Mediatrix of All Graces® Icon was very specially honored in SAINT PETER'S BASILICA by being placed at the altar, in a Solemn Mass, concelebrated by 24 Archbishops and Bishops IN THE HEART OF SAINT PETER'S BASILICA DIRECTLY IN FRONT OF SAINT PETER'S TOMB! This Sacred Mary Mediatrix Icon was also greatly honored to be at the Altar during Mass in "The Grotto of the Popes", under Saint Peter's Basilica Main Altar – where nearly all of the 264 popes are buried.

33. On May 13, 1999, the Original Icon of "Our Lady Mediatrix of All Graces" was at the Altar during Holy Mass in Saint Mary Major Papal Basilica in Rome, on The Feast Day of Our Lady of Fatima, May 13, 1999. This Papal Basilica is the first, the largest and most important Basilica to Mary in the world!

34. On May 13, of that same year, the Sacred Mary Mediatrix Icon was greatly honored to be in the second largest church in the world, SAINT PAUL OUTSIDE THE WALLS PAPAL BASILICA in front of the Tomb of Saint Paul the Apostle at the immense main Altar, at a Special Mass, concelebrated by 24 Archbishops and Bishops!

35. Also on the Feast Day of Our Lady of Fatima, May 13, 1999, the Fatima-related Icon, Our Lady Mediatrix of All Graces® was at the main Altar, at Mass in SAINT JOHN LATERAN PAPAL BASILICA with 24 Archbishops and Bishops.

36. On May 14, 1999, Pope John Paul II specially blessed the original Sacred Icon of Our Lady Mediatrix of All Graces with Mary's very powerful role as "Our Lady Mediatrix of All of God's Graces"! This historic Private Audience was in the Pope's Personal Office and Library in the Vatican. After the Pope's discussion about this Sacred Icon, he pointed out details in the Icon! The Pope then said: "... Bring the Icon to my Chapel in my residence, and place the Icon next to the Altar for the Papal Mass" and for prayers before Our Lady Mediatrix Icon"! This Papal Mass was concelebrated with 26 Archbishops and Bishops! The Pope very gratefully received: 3 large Icons of "Our Lady Mediatrix of all Graces ..." our "Mediatrix Icon Book", our "Mary Mediatrix 'Prayer Cards'", and our exquisite "Icon Medal" of "Our Lady Mediatrix of All Graces" for his use! His Holiness, Pope John Paul II showed his appreciation for his "Mary Mediatrix" gifts, and for this meeting, by giving a "Custom-made Papal Rosary" with his "Papal Crucifix" and his "Papal coat-of-Arms" on it and also on a leather-bound, satin lined, "Papal Rosary Case" with his Papal Coat-of-Arms inside!

37. On May 16, 1999, the Sacred, original "Mary Mediatrix Icon" was placed on the right rear side of Pope John Paul II's temporary Outdoor Altar at the top of the steps, directly in front of Saint Peter's Basilica, for the outdoor Sunday Papal Mass with over 300,000 people in attendance

38. On November 26 and 27, 2001, the Patriarch of the Russian Orthodox Church, Archbishop of Moscow, Archbishop John Bereslavsky with 100 Russian Orthodox Bishops, and Priests, through the Russian Orthodox Church, together with thousands of Russian people consecrated all of Russia, Ukraine, Belarus, and Moldova and consecrated themselves to the "Immaculate Heart of Mary" through Our Lady Mediatrix of All Graces Icon in Moscow, Russia!

39. On December 8, 2001, on the Feast Day of "The Immaculate Conception", Josyp Terelya brought a video tape and 200 photographs of "The Consecration of Russia, through the Russian Orthodox Church, through Our Lady Mediatrix of All Graces Icon" to Pope John Paul II in a Private Audience in Rome. After his private audience with Pope John Paul II, Josyp Terelya called Francis Slinsky, the Founder and Director of Mary's Way and said: "Holy Father had tears of overwhelming joy streaming from his eyes for 6 to 7 minutes while he carefully studied every one of the 200 photographs of the Consecration of Russia and people, through the Russian Orthodox Church to Mary through the 'Our Lady Mediatrix of All Graces Icon'!"

40. On March 25, 2002, on the Feast Day of "The Annunciation", the Original Miraculous Icon® of Our Lady Mediatrix of All Graces® Icon was blessed with

the Precious Blood of Jesus with an "All-Healing and An All evil-dispelling Icon Blessing," at the altar during Holy Mass, in The Orthodox Catholic Church Rite. Benedictine Priest, Father Miguel DeMaria Rosa Mistica, O.S.B. touched the Miracle of the Precious Blood of Jesus on the Purificator to the Kissing Lips of Jesus and Mary, on the Original Miraculous Icon, Our Lady Mediatrix of All Graces!

70

The following is from Father David explaining the vitally important dream he had on August 5th, 2010 the Feast Day of Our Lady of Snows which is also Our Lady's Birthday! "I had a dream in which the Blessed Mother appeared to me with your Brown Scapulars in her outstretched hands. BLESSED MOTHER SAID TO ME: 'WHOEVER WEARS THE SCAPULAR WILL BE PROTECTED - AND SAVED! A LOT OF PEOPLE WILL BE SAVED WITH THIS SCAPULAR'! It was the reason why I called you. Blessed Mother showed me your scapulars IN BOTH OF HER OUTSTREACHED HANDS!" Father David continued - "Blessed Mother put all this together – to make connections. Amazing how Blessed Mother put this all together! This man Francis tried to make these Scapulars for 10 years. Amazing! With Our Lady Mediatrix of All Graces – Very Good! And also with Saint Michael the Archangel – Very Perfect! Nobody does this: nobody touches Scapulars to all these relics –which is Perfect! These Scapulars are purified and helping people who wear them. A LOT OF MIRACLES WILL HAPPEN", FATHER DAVID SAID!

"In this dream of August 5th I said to myself 'my God, what is this!' I'd never seen this image of the Blessed Virgin Mary before! When I awoke that morning I began asking people around me; The Bishop; The Monsignor. I called Father Gabriele Amorth in Vatican City who is my Spiritual Director and who is also the Chief Exorcist for the Vatican. He taught me exorcism, how to exorcise people. I told Father Amorth of the dream of the Blessed Virgin Mary holding these scapulars in her hands. Father Amorth reminded me what the then retired (now deceased) Cardinal Secretary of State to Pope John Paul II, Cardinal Agostino Casaroli told him about this Icon in 1997. Cardinal Casaroli wrote a document in 1997 about this Icon of "Our Lady Mediatrix of All Graces" when Francis was in Rome at an international conference with the original Icon on stage with over 200 world leaders. He also wrote about Francis Slinsky the Icon's originator. Father David said that Cardinal Casaroli gave him information many years ago about the Our Lady Mediatrix of All Graces Icon but that he lost the document. This Document miraculously appeared in my chapel near his altar the next morning after being lost for 14 years! When Father David miraculously found this document next to his altar the next morning after his morning Mass, it explained all about the Icon and about the Icons owner and originator Francis Slinsky. It said that Francis Slinsky a very special person is deep in religion. It had your old obsolete telephone number on it which somehow mysteriously still worked. I asked Bernadette in the United States to call you and find out something about Our Lady Mediatrix of All Graces Scapulars. It was amazing!"

NOTE: *Father David will offer Masses for you and your entire family: your wife, your husband, all your children, your mother, your Father, all your brothers and sisters, all your nieces and nephews, all your grandparents, all living and all deceased relatives, your entire family tree on both sides of your family, etc.! This helps provide funds for Father's orphanages with over 500 very needy orphan children. Every morning for one year, two Traditional Latin Rite Masses will be offered for you and your entire family: one by Father David, a miracle working Capuchin priest who has stigmata wounds on his hands, which Pope John Paul II witnessed and acknowledged and which was also confirmed by the Vatican's physician. A second Latin Rite Mass will also be said for you and your family by a Franciscan priest in the Holy Land.*

Every evening for one year, two 1½ hour long Gregorian Masses sung with Gregorian chants in two monasteries, concluding with two Eucharistic processions and adoration will also be offered for you and your family: one Gregorian Mass by priests who assist Father David, and a second Gregorian Mass by Franciscan priest in the holy land. The Gregorian Masses and Eucharistic procession and adoration which last for three hours every night for a year are also offered up for you and for your entire family.

Your intentions and the intentions of your entire immediate family – living and deceased - will be offered in four holy Masses every day for one year for total of 1,460 Masses. These 1,460 Masses are offered through The Blessed Mother's most powerful role as "Our Lady Mediatrix of All Graces" which is a doctrine of the Catholic Church.

Mary Mediatrix of All Graces, as Queen of Heaven and Mother of God, presents all your personal, spiritual, physical, emotional and financial needs, and all the needs of your entire family directly to her Son Jesus, through these Masses and rosaries every day. These Masses are for the spiritual, physical, emotional and financial needs of your entire family.

Father David and his priests and religious sisters who work in his orphanages will also pray 35 rosaries for you and for your entire family's intentions every day for one year - a total of 12,775 rosaries!

Your donation for these 1,460 very holy masses and 12,775 rosaries offered through the Blessed Mother's most powerful role as "Our Lady Mediatrix of All God's Graces" helps support Father David's vital work at his orphanages for his 505 orphaned children - many of whom are very sickly.

For your donation, for the 1,460 Masses and 12,775 Rosaries offered for all of your intentions and for the intentions of your all your family members, or for any other purpose, we will also send you a beautiful Mass card with The Miraculous Icon Our Lady Mediatrix of All Graces – a Doctrine of the Church on the outside. On the inside of this Mass Card are 2 photos taken in the 1950's of Padre Pio with then 3 year old David, and Padre Pio giving a Holy Card to a then 7 year David (who later became Capuchin Father David with the Stigmata who now offers your Masses) at young David's First Communion! Padre Pio was also David's Sponsor at David's Confirmation! Young David, who then became a Capuchin priest was with Padre Pio for 16 years. The third side has the information about your Masses and rosaries signed by Father David with his Seal of Office. The fourth side has a photograph of Father David very intently praying for the people he says Masses for and offers many rosaries for on Apparition Hill in Medjugorje at the 3 o'clock Divine Mercy Hour – where 4 wonderful miracles happened and are shown in this astonishing photograph which was given to Saint Pope John Paul II.

Enroll now to have 730 Traditional Latin Masses and 730 Gregorian Masses 1,460 total Masses and 12,775 rosaries offered for you and your family's intentions go to http://www.marysway.net/730-masses-by-stigmata-priest-for-intentions/.

Father is very busy throughout each day. He says his Traditional Latin Rite Mass every morning for people who request Masses be said by him for donations for his many orphan children and for his monastery at 6:00 o'clock each morning. He helps his workers take care of and feed his orphan children each morning. He helps feed the homeless at lunch time and also feed the homeless at dinner time. He visits the hospitals each day to pray over sick people and to bring comfort to them. After dinner he looks for children in the streets who are hungry and abandoned. They live in the sewer systems. The fumes from the sewers keep the children warm. They inhaled these fumes all the time. They spend each day begging for scraps of food or eat the rotten food they find in garbage cans and in food dumps. They then sleep in dirt gutters, in the woods, in parks, in abandoned houses anywhere they can find shelter. They sleep on and under old newspapers and old cardboard to keep them warm. Father always looks on river banks where people throw their infants into the rivers to drown and they land on river banks and starve to death there. Father's been fighting with the government of these countries about this for years. The governments say is not our problem. Father David says "Yes, it is your problem because these children belong to you and to me. The governments say they cannot do anything about it." Father says "They only want to enrich themselves."

To help Father David and his more than 500 orphan children and to help you and your family please enroll now to have 730 Traditional Latin Masses and 730 Gregorian Masses a total of 1,460 Masses said for you and your family for the year by Father David. Also, Father and his workers at his orphanages will pray 35 rosaries each day for you and your families intentions a total of 12,275 rosaries each year. We will send you a Mass card stating this and signed by Father David with his seal of office on it. Go to our website http://www.marysway.net/730–masses-by-stigmata-priest-for-intentions/.

CHAPTER 12
THREE DAYS OF DARKNESS

The Three Days of Total Darkness
Our Lord to Padre Pio

Translation of a copy of a personal letter written by Padre Pio address to the Commission of Heroldsbach appointed by the Vatican which testifies to the truth and reality of these revelations given by Our Lord to Padre Pio, a Capuchin priest who bore the stigmata.

New Year's Eve 1949- Jesus: "My son, My son, I have been longing for this hour in which I again shall reveal to you the great love of My heart. My love for man is very great, especially for those who give themselves to Me. They are My refuge and My Consolation in the many and terrible irreverence which I receive in the Sacrament of My love.

"Pray and make reparation to Me. Admonish others to do the same because the time is near at hand in which I shall visit my unfaithful people because they have not heeded the time of My grace. Persevere in prayer, so that your adversary shall have no dominion over you. Tell My people to be prepared at all times, for My judgment shall come upon them suddenly and when least expected- and not one shall escape My hands. I shall find them all! I shall protect the just. Watch the sun and moon and the stars of Heaven- when they appear to be unduly disturbed and restless, know that the day is not far away, Stay united in prayer and watching until the angel of destruction has passed your doors. Pray that these days will be shortened.

"My beloved, have confidence. I am in the midst of you. My kingdom shall be glorified and My Name shall be blessed from the rising of the sun unto the setting thereof; and to My Kingdom there shall be no end."

January 23, 1950

"Pray! Make reparation! Be fervent and practice mortifications. Great things are at stake! Pray! Men are running toward the abyss of Hell in great rejoicing and merry making, as though they were going to a masquerade ball or the wedding feast of the devil himself! Assist Me in the salvation of souls. The measure of sin is filled! The day of revenge, with its terrifying happenings is near! Nearer than you can imagine! And the world is sleeping in false security! The divine judgment shall strike them like a thunderbolt! These godless and wicked people shall be destroyed without mercy, as were the inhabitants of Sodom and Gomorra of old. Yes, I tell you, their wickedness was not as great as that of our human race of today!"

January 28, 1950

"Keep your windows well covered. Do not look out. Light a blessed candle, which will suffice for many days. Pray the Rosary. Read spiritual books. Make acts of Spiritual Communion also acts of love, which are so pleasing to Us. Pray with outstretched arms, or prostrate on the ground, in order that many souls may be saved. Do not go outside the house. Provide yourself with sufficient food. The powers of nature shall be moved and a rain of fire shall make people tremble with fear. Have courage. I am in the midst of you."

February 7, 1950

"Take care of the animals during these days. I am the Creator and Preserver of all animals as well as man. I shall give you a few signs before hand at which time you should place more food before them. I will preserve the property of the elect, including the animals, for they shall be in need of sustenance afterwards as well. Let no one go across the yard, even to feed the animals- he who steps outside will perish! Cover your windows carefully. My elect shall not see My wrath. Have confidence in Me, and I will be your protection, your confidence obliges Me to come to your aid.

"The hour of My coming is near! But I will show mercy. A most dreadful punishment will bear witness to the times. My angels, who are to be the executioners of this work, are ready with their pointed swords! They will take a special care to annihilate all these who mocked Me and would not believe in My revelations.

"Hurricanes of fire will pour forth from the clouds and spread over the entire earth! Storms, bad weather, thunderbolts and earthquakes will cover the earth for two days. An uninterrupted rain of fire will take place! It will begin during a very cold night. All this is to prove that God is the Master of Creation.
"Those who hope in Me, and believe in my words, have nothing to fear because I will not forsake them, nor those who are in the state of grace and who seek My mother's protection.

"That you may be prepared for these visitations, I will give you the following signs and instructions: The night will be very cold. The wind will roar. After

114

a time, thunderbolts will be heard. Lock all the doors and windows. Talk to no one outside the house. Kneel down before a crucifix, be sorry for your sins, and beg My Mother's protection. Do not look during the earthquake, because the anger of God is holy!" Jesus does not want us to behold the anger of God, because God's anger must be contemplated with fear and trembling.

"Those who disregard this advice will be killed instantly. The wind will carry with it the poisonous gases which will be diffused over the entire earth. Those who suffer and die innocently will be martyrs and they will be with Me in My Kingdom.

"Satan will triumph! But in three nights, the earthquake and fire will cease. On the following day the sun will shine again, angels will descend from Heaven and will spread the spirit of peace over the earth. A feeling of immeasurable gratitude will take possession of those who survive the impending punishment, this most terrible ordeal since creation, with which God will visit the earth. "

"I have chosen souls in other countries too, such as Belgium, Switzerland, Spain, who have received these revelations so that other countries also may be prepared. Pray the Rosary, but pray it well, so that your prayers may reach Heaven. Soon a more terrible catastrophe shall come upon the entire world, such as has never been witnessed before, a terrible chastisement never before experienced!

"How unconcerned men are regarding these things which shall so soon come upon them, contrary to all expectations. How indifferent they are in preparing themselves for these unheard of events, through which they will have to pass so shortly!

"The weight of the Divine balance has reached the earth! The wrath of My Father shall be poured out over the entire world! I am again warning the world through your instrumentality, as I have so often done heretofore.

"The sins of men have multiplied beyond measure: Irreverence in church, sinful pride committed in sham religious activities, lack of true brotherly love, indecency in dress, especially at summer resorts. The world is filled with iniquity.

"This catastrophe shall come upon the earth like a flash of lightening at which moment the light of the morning sun shall be replaced by black darkness! No one shall leave the house or look out of a window from that moment on. I myself shall come amidst thunder and lightning. The wicked shall behold My Divine Heart. There shall be great confusion because of this utter darkness in which the entire earth shall be enveloped, and many, many shall die from fear and despair.

"Those who shall fight for My cause shall receive grace from My Divine Heart; and the cry, "WHO IS LIKE UNTO GOD!" shall serve as a means of protection to many. However, many shall burn in the open fields like withered grass! The godless shall be annihilated, so that afterwards the just shall be able to start (different word-stand) afresh.

"On that day, as soon as complete darkness has set in, no one shall leave the house or look out of the window. The darkness shall last a day and a night, followed by another day and a night, and another day- but in the night following, the stars will shine again, and on the next morning the sun shall rise again, and it will be springtime!

"In the days of darkness, My elect shall not sleep, as did the disciples in the Garden of Olives. They shall pray incessantly, and they shall not be disappointed in Me. I shall gather My elect. Hell will believe itself to be in possession of the entire earth, but I shall reclaim it.

"Do you, perhaps, think that I would permit My Father to have such terrible chastisements come upon the world, if the world would turn from iniquity to justice? But because of My great love, these afflictions shall be permitted to come upon man. Although many shall curse Me, yet thousands of souls shall be saved through them. No human understanding can fathom the depth of my love!

"Pray! Pray! I desire your prayers. My dear Mother Mary, Saint Joseph, Saint Elizabeth, Saint Conrad, Saint Michael, Saint Peter, the Little Theresa, Your Holy Angels, shall be your intercessors. Implore their aid! Be courageous soldiers of Christ! At the return of light, let everyone give thanks to the Hold Trinity for Their Protection! The devastation shall be very great! But I, your God, will have purified the earth. I am with you. Have confidence!

CHAPTER 13
OUR LADY OF LA SALETTE

"On September 19, 1846, Maximin Giraud and Mélanie Calvat reported seeing the Virgin Mary on Mount Sous-Les Baisses, weeping bitterly. According to their account, she continued to weep even as she spoke to them—first in French, then in their own dialect. After speaking, the apparition vanished. The following day the children's account of the apparition was put into writing and signed by the visionaries and those who had heard the story.

According to the children's account, the Virgin invited people to respect the repose of Sunday, and the name of God. She threatened punishment, in particular a scarcity of potatoes, which would rot. The context of these punishments places the warning just prior to the winter of 1846-1847, which was in Europe, and especially in Ireland and in France, a period of famine in the months which followed the apparition. This was one of the factors of the apparition's popular appeal.

After five years of research, the bishop of Grenoble, Philibert de Bruillard recognized the authenticity of the apparition and Pope Pius IX approved the devotion to Our Lady of La Salette.

The children also reported that the Blessed Virgin had confided a special secret to each of them. These two secrets, which neither Melanie or Maximin ever made known to each other, were sent by them in 1851 to Pope Pius IX on the advice of Mgr. de Bruillard.

Mélanie first recorded her revealed Secret on July 3, in Corenc, at the Sisters of Providence residence and it was carried to the Bishop's House. She was asked to rewrite her Secret on July 6. Then the Bishop read the document before sealing it. Mélanie's statement was: 'Secret which the Blessed Virgin gave me on the Mountain of La Salette on September 19, 1846.'

Mélanie, I will say something to you which you will not say to anybody:

The time of the God's wrath has arrived! If, when you say to the people what

I have said to you so far, and what I will still ask you to say, if, after that, they do not convert, (if they do not do penance, and they do not cease working on Sunday, and if they continue to blaspheme the Holy Name of God), in a word, if the face of the earth does not change, God will be avenged against the people ungrateful and slave of the demon.

My Son will make his power manifest! Paris, this city soiled by all kinds of crimes, will perish infallibly. Marseilles will be destroyed in a little time. When these things arrive, the disorder will be complete on the earth, the world will be given up to its impious passions.

The pope will be persecuted from all sides, they will shoot at him, they will want to put him to death, but no one will be able to do it, the Vicar of God will triumph again this time.

The priests and the Sisters, and the true servants of my Son will be persecuted, and several will die for the faith of Jesus Christ.

A famine will reign at the same time.

After all these will have arrived, many will recognize the hand of God on them, they will convert, and do penance for their sins.

A great king will go up on the throne, and will reign a few years. Religion will re-flourish and spread all over the world, and there will be a great abundance, the world, glad not to be lacking nothing, will fall again in its disorders, will give up God, and will be prone to its criminal passions.

Among God's ministers, and the Spouses of Jesus-Christ, there will be some who will go astray, and that will be the most terrible.

Lastly, hell will reign on earth. It will be then that the Antichrist will be born of a Sister, but woe to her! Many will believe in him, because he will claim to have come from heaven, woe to those who will believe in him!

That time is not far away, twice 50 years will not go by.

My child, you will not say what I have just said to you. (You will not say it to anybody, you will not say if you must say it one day, you will not say what that it concerns), finally you will say nothing anymore until I tell you to say it!

I pray to Our Holy Father the Pope to give me his holy blessing.

~ *Mélanie Mathieu, Shepherdess of La Salette, Grenoble, July 6, 1851*

Maximin Giraud wrote his revealed Secret at the bishop's palace, in front of Bishop de Bruillard's staff on July 3, 1851 in the evening. He was asked to rewrite it again because of spots of ink. The Secret was delivered to the bishop sent to the pope. The sealed envelope was countersigned by two witnesses. Giraud's statement was:

Here is the secret of Maximin written in 1851 that was never revealed until 1999:

On September 19, 1846, we saw a beautiful Lady. We never said that this lady was the Blessed Virgin but we always said that it was a beautiful Lady. I do not know if it is the Blessed Virgin or another person. As for me, I believe today that it is the Blessed Virgin. Here is what this Lady said to me:

"If my people continue, what I will say to you will arrive earlier, if it changes a little, it will be a little later.

France has corrupted the universe, one day it will be punished. The faith will die out in France: three quarters of France will not practice religion anymore, or almost no more, the other part will practice it without really practicing it. Then, after that, nations will convert, the faith will be rekindled everywhere. A great country, now Protestant, in the north of Europe, will be converted; by the support of this country all the other nations of the world will be converted.

Before all that arrives, great disorders will arrive, in the Church, and everywhere. Then, after that, our Holy Father the Pope will be persecuted. His successor will be a pontiff that nobody expects.

Then, after that, a great peace will come, but it will not last a long time. A monster will come to disturb it. All that I tell you here will arrive in the other century, at the latest in the year two thousand."

She told me to say it sometime before.

~ *Maximin Giraud Grenoble, July 3, 1851*

Saint John Paul II stated: "As I wrote on the occasion of the 150th anniversary, 'La Salette is a message of hope, for our hope is nourished by the intercession of her who is the Mother of mankind.'"

The message of the visionaries of La Salette focuses on the conversion of all humanity to Christ. Though La Salette's message is embedded in the bygone environment of the nineteenth century, rural France, it has had a tremendous impact on the modern world. Saints (for example, John Vianney), pastors (such as Don Bosco), and religious writers have all been influenced by La Salette. The spirit of La Salette is one of prayer, conversion, and commitment.

La Salette - Authentic Documents, Volumes I-III,
compiled by Fr. Jean Stern, the archivist of the Missionaries of Our Lady of La Salette in Rome